Alan Titchmarsh
how to garden

Flowering Shrubs

Alan Titchmarsh
how to garden

Flowering
Shrubs

BOOKS

Published in 2010 by BBC Books, an imprint of
Ebury Publishing, a Random House Group Company

The Random House Group Limited Reg. No. 954009

Addresses for companies within the Random House
Group can be found at
www.randomhouse.co.uk

The Random House Group Limited supports The Forest
Stewardship Council (FSC), the leading international
forest certification organisation. All our titles that are
printed on Greenpeace approved FSC certified paper
carry the FSC logo. Our paper procurement policy can
be found at www.rbooks.co.uk/environment

A CIP catalogue record for this book is available from
the British Library.

ISBN 978 1 84 6074028

Produced by OutHouse!
Shalbourne, Marlborough, Wiltshire SN8 3QJ

BBC BOOKS
COMMISSIONING EDITOR: Lorna Russell
PROJECT EDITOR: Caroline McArthur
PRODUCTION: Phil Spencer

OUTHOUSE!
CONCEPT DEVELOPMENT & SERIES DESIGN:
    Elizabeth Mallard-Shaw, Sharon Cluett
PROJECT MANAGEMENT: Polly Boyd, Sue Gordon
ART DIRECTOR: Robin Whitecross
CONTRIBUTING EDITOR: Jonathan Edwards
PROJECT EDITOR: Bella Pringle
DESIGNERS: Louise Turpin, Heather McCarry

ILLUSTRATIONS by Lizzie Harper except pages 40–42,
which are by Julia Brittain

PHOTOGRAPHS by Jonathan Buckley except where
credited otherwise on page 128

Colour origination by Altaimage, London
Printed and bound by Firmengruppe APPL,
Wemding, Germany

Contents

Introduction	7
INTRODUCING FLOWERING SHRUBS	8
What are flowering shrubs?	9
Using flowering shrubs	10
focus on Shrubs for wildlife	16
Shrubs in tubs	18
Designing with flowering shrubs	20
focus on Scent	22
Structure and form	23
focus on Tree-like shrubs	26
Combining colours	28
focus on Evergreen shrubs for year-round interest	33
Shrubs with other plants	36
Planning a border	40
Plants for a purpose	43

PLANTING AND GROWING	**46**	**SHRUBS FOR CHALLENGING SITES**	**108**
Tools and equipment	47	Dense shade	109
Growing conditions	48	Steep slopes and banks	110
Choosing flowering shrubs	50	Hot, dry spots	111
Planting flowering shrubs	51	Sandy soil	112
Moving established shrubs	54	Clay soil	113
Watering	55	**focus on** Wind tunnels and frost pockets	114
Feeding	56	Wet conditions	115
Weed control and mulching	57	Acidic soil	116
focus on Winter protection	59	Chalky soil	117
Pruning	60		
focus on Growing a flowering shrub as a standard	66	**SEASON BY SEASON**	**118**
Propagation	67	Spring	119
Plant problems and remedies	72	Summer	121
		Autumn	122
RECOMMENDED FLOWERING SHRUBS	**76**	Winter	123
A–Z directory	77	Index	124

Introduction

Gardening is one of the best and most fulfilling activities on earth, but it can sometimes seem complicated and confusing. The answers to problems can usually be found in books, but big fat gardening books can be rather daunting. Where do you start? How can you find just the information you want without wading through lots of stuff that is not appropriate to your particular problem? Well, a good index is helpful, but sometimes a smaller book devoted to one particular subject fits the bill better – especially if it is reasonably priced and if you have a small garden where you might not be able to fit in everything suggested in a larger volume.

The *How to Garden* books aim to fill that gap – even if sometimes it may be only a small one. They are clearly set out and written, I hope, in a straightforward, easy-to-understand style. I don't see any point in making gardening complicated, when much of it is based on common sense and observation. (All the key techniques are explained and illustrated, and I've included plenty of tips and tricks of the trade.)

There are suggestions on the best plants and the best varieties to grow in particular situations and for a particular effect. I've tried to keep the information crisp and to the point so that you can find what you need quickly and easily and then put your new-found knowledge into practice. Don't worry if you're not familiar with the Latin names of plants. They are there to make sure you can find the plant as it will be labelled in the nursery or garden centre, but where appropriate I have included common names, too. Forgetting a plant's name need not stand in your way when it comes to being able to grow it.

Above all, the *How to Garden* books are designed to fill you with passion and enthusiasm for your garden and all that its creation and care entails, from designing and planting it to maintaining it and enjoying it. For more than fifty years gardening has been my passion, and that initial enthusiasm for watching plants grow, for trying something new and for just being outside pottering has never faded. If anything I am keener on gardening now than I ever was and get more satisfaction from my plants every day. It's not that I am simply a romantic, but rather that I have learned to look for the good in gardens and in plants, and there is lots to be found. Oh, there are times when I fail – when my plants don't grow as well as they should and I need to try harder. But where would I rather be on a sunny day? Nowhere!

The *How to Garden* handbooks will, I hope, allow some of that enthusiasm – childish though it may be – to rub off on you, and the information they contain will, I hope, make you a better gardener, as well as opening your eyes to the magic of plants and flowers.

Introducing flowering shrubs

Flowering shrubs are among the most rewarding of garden plants. In the main they're easy to grow, with plenty of examples that need very little maintenance. A clever mix of evergreen and deciduous shrubs will fill beds and borders with bold shapes, attractive foliage and spectacular flowers, and will offer a continually changing display throughout the year. Forming the structural backbone of any good planting scheme, they are permanent additions to the garden, performing reliably for many years.

What are flowering shrubs?

Shrubs are a large and varied group of garden plants with woody stems, which do not die back each year. Most shrubs naturally produce a bushy shape, and many are multi-stemmed, distinguishing them from trees, which generally have a single stem. The shrubs that bear flowers are some of the most beautiful and useful of plants and, being permanent, should form the framework of a planting scheme. Their size and shape, as well as whether they are evergreen or deciduous, determine how best to use them, as do their flowering time, fragrance and whether they produce fruits or rich autumn foliage.

Great garden value and very easy to grow, *Potentilla fruticosa* 'Red Ace' flowers all summer long.

Shrubs put on a certain amount of growth each year, which thickens and is built on the next year. Most shrubs reach around 4–8m (13–26ft) in height, but there are numerous exceptions, with the smallest barely getting off the ground and the tallest touching 15m (49ft).

Just to confuse you, there are some tall, upright shrubs that reach tree-like proportions (*see* pages 26–7). And a few trees lend themselves to being trained with several stems, so that they look like shrubs ... which does blur the distinction between trees and shrubs somewhat!

Star performers
Flowering shrubs have the edge over other members of the shrub family in that while having an all-year presence, there is a 'golden period' when they're in bloom. Their flowers are as varied in shape and size as the shrubs that bear them. They come in every colour of the spectrum, and are produced in every season of the year, some of them lasting for months on end.

Many flowering shrubs also offer delightful fragrance, adding another dimension to the pleasure a garden can give, not just during the summer but in the depths of winter, too. What's more, the blooms of some of these shrubs are followed in autumn by abundant crops of colourful fruits, loved by the birds, while others are noted for their dazzling autumn foliage tints.

A heartlifting stalwart that flowers in early spring, *Kerria japonica* is ideal for dappled shade under a tree.

Using flowering shrubs

With such a diversity of shape and form, as well as a truly dazzling range of flowers and foliage, flowering shrubs are a key ingredient in all successful garden designs. Their most important contribution is providing permanent structure – the framework that every garden requires – but they perform many other functions, too. Thinking about these will help you select the right plants from what might seem a bewildering choice.

The garden skeleton

Every garden, large or small, rural or urban, needs to have a basic structure. This is what shrubs and trees provide – a permanent backbone of planting. Get this right and everything else will fall into place.

Whether they're deciduous or evergreen, dwarf and spreading, low and mound-forming, or tall and upright, shrubs form a framework on which everything else hangs. They should stand out from the 'fillers' that flesh out the bones (bulbs, annuals and herbaceous perennials), giving a sense of continuity from one season and one year to the next.

Evergreens might seem the most obvious structural plants, but deciduous flowering shrubs can also make a significant contribution to the overall garden picture, even in winter, after their leaves have fallen and the distinctive pattern of their branches is revealed.

Many flowering shrubs make excellent specimen plants, and can be used as a dramatic point of focus when in flower. A plant like this can stand alone in a lawn or gravelled area, or be incorporated into a border, performing a key role in the structural plan of the garden.

Mixed borders

In the days of large gardens, when there were teams of people to do the work, shrubs were frequently

In mid- to late summer, hydrangeas provide colour and structure to this mixed planting in semi-shade, as they jostle cheek-by-jowl with herbaceous perennials, hardy ferns and bulbs.

In an exposed spot, a backdrop of wind-tolerant shrubs provides shelter for the stunning flowers of rhododendrons, set off by a frilly skirt of variegated hostas.

grown in a dedicated border, or 'shrubbery'. Today, most flowering shrubs are found in mixed borders, rubbing up against other types of plants, typically herbaceous perennials, annuals and bulbs. Plants with contrasting foliage and flowers, and different flowering periods, are combined to create a continuous succession of interest within the border, throughout the year.

When thinking about how to use flowering shrubs in a border, it can make the whole process a lot less daunting if you break the planting down into three different levels. Think about what might cover the ground, below eye level; what could be the mid-storey plants, at eye level; and what might be used to stand out at the back of the border, above eye level, to create the skyline.

Some low-growing flowering shrubs make good understorey plants beneath larger shrubs and trees, forming knee-deep ground cover, which will provide interest and also help to keep down weeds (*see* pages 14–15). Many flowering shrubs form rounded dome shapes and make excellent fillers in the middle of a mixed border. Others are much more upright, like mahonia, or fountain-shaped, like buddleia, forsythia or philadelphus – all useful further back in the border.

One bonus of using shrubs in a mixed border is that by combining them with other types of plant you can find sheltered spots for the 'not-so-hardy' plants to nestle in among their more robust neighbours. Another plus point is that a mixed border requires less maintenance than an equivalent-sized herbaceous border, so is a good option if time, or inclination, is limited.

Don't forget

Bear in mind that perennials and bulbs will need lifting and dividing from time to time, so you should leave space for access in the border. Be very careful not to disturb the roots of the shrubs while you carry out this task.

Take advantage of a warm, sheltered wall to grow a borderline-hardy shrub, such as evergreen *Ceanothus* 'Concha', that might not survive elsewhere.

Screens and windbreaks

By carefully placing wind-tolerant flowering shrubs, you can provide shelter for less-than-robust shrubs. Even some otherwise hardy flowering shrubs can be vulnerable to damage at certain times. For example, the young shoots of *Halesia carolina* and dwarf rhododendrons and azaleas can all be damaged by winds early in the growing season, and would benefit from extra protection at this time.

The most effective windbreak filters the wind (rather than blocking its path, like a wall or fence does), so flowering shrubs are ideal. In a large garden you can mix wind-tolerant flowering shrubs with trees to create a shelter belt, while in a small garden, flowering evergreens and bamboos will do the trick.

Nearly all gardens benefit from wind protection. Even in seemingly sheltered urban gardens, the wind can whistle through gaps between buildings. The damage caused by wind tunnels between buildings can be limited by planting wind-tolerant shrubs at either end of the passage. In an exposed garden, you can plant either the whole boundary with wind-tolerant shrubs, to form a windbreak to protect the entire site, or you can place them strategically within the garden, to create sheltered planting pockets for more tender specimens. The best to try are *Cotoneaster simonsii*, *Erica arborea*, rosemary, *Santolina chamaecyparissus* and *Viburnum tinus* (*see also* page 114). In mild coastal areas, salt-tolerant flowering shrubs such as *Escallonia* 'Apple Blossom' work well as a protective hedge.

Hedges and dividers

Several flowering shrubs make excellent hedges. Choose robust, bushy, densely growing shrubs, preferably evergreen. If they have spines on their stems or prickly leaves they'll provide an efficient intruder-deterrent too. For example, you could plant the prickly barberry

Fuchsia magellanica makes a spectacular informal flowering garden divider all summer long, but needs a sheltered, mild site as it is only borderline-hardy.

(*Berberis thunbergii*) or flowering quince (*Chaenomeles*).

If you want a fairly formal hedge, the shrubs will need to be pruned regularly and ideally have twiggy stems that grow together to create a continuous barrier, like escallonia. Bear in mind that you'll have to sacrifice a lot of the flowering potential of shrubs if they are trimmed more formally. If the flowering hedge also produces berries, delay trimming and tidying up until winter. If you have the space, however, flowering shrubs can be used to create an informal hedge, so that you can enjoy their flowers and fruit, too.

For an unusual and striking boundary, you could try creating a mixed hedge from two or more varieties of flowering shrub. It's important to select those that bloom at the same time so that they can be pruned simultaneously, just after flowering. Similarly, yellow- and red-berrying pyracantha varieties can be used to create two-tone blocks of autumn hedge colour.

Within the garden itself, you can use some low-growing flowering shrubs to define paths or borders, or to divide the garden into 'rooms'. English lavender (*Lavandula*) and the compact rosemary *Rosmarinus officinalis* 'Majorca Pink' are ideal for this purpose. In a mild, sheltered garden you have a greater choice of

A narrow mixed border is backed by the cream-coloured flowers of philadelphus (mock orange), which dramatically increases the impact of the display.

plants and can include borderline-hardy shrubs, such as the striking *Fuchsia magellanica* (*see* opposite).

Backdrops for borders

Larger shrubs can be used at the back of a border to act as a foil for the plants in front when they are performing, and to provide seasonal interest when they are not. For a narrow border, choose spectacular spring or early summer flowering shrubs, *Philadelphus* 'Belle Etoile' perhaps, that will really make a show before other plants get going.

For larger borders, include some winter-flowering shrubs such as *Viburnum × bodnantense* 'Charles Lamont', as well as those that bear autumn crops of fruit, like pyracantha, or have striking evergreen foliage. Their displays should come to prominence just as plants that flower in the main season start to fade.

Taller shrubs at the back of a border can be used to perform another valuable function, and that is blurring the boundaries – which has the effect of making your garden seem bigger than it actually is.

USING FLOWERING SHRUBS **13**

Fremontodendron 'California Glory' is an excellent choice for training against a sheltered, sunny wall that is protected from cold winds.

Filling gaps

Several fast-growing flowering shrubs make good gap-fillers. For the back of the border, consider quick-growing shrubs like buddleias, brooms (*Cytisus*), kerrias, *Leycesteria formosa,* the mallow *Lavatera × clementii* 'Barnsley', and hardy fuchsias, such as 'Riccartonii'. The buddleia, fuchsia, lavatera and leycesteria can be pruned back hard each year, after flowering, if you want to keep them small. Another option for fillers are shrubs that transplant well. *Potentilla fruticosa* 'Elizabeth', for example, is happy to be moved whenever necessary.

Growing against walls

A few shrubs, known as wall shrubs, are well suited to training against vertical surfaces. This has become such a popular way of growing some hardy flowering shrubs, including flowering quince (*Chaenomeles*), that you rarely see them grown as freestanding specimens. This is because the vertical training shows off their decorative features to best effect and helps overcome their natural tendency to sprawl. Less-than-hardy shrubs also benefit when

Heathers make great little humps of ground cover. Here, the mounds are accentuated by the contrasting acid-green colour and upright habit of a single conifer.

grown against the warmth of a sheltered wall. Sites like this allow you to grow a wider range of tender shrubs than would otherwise be possible. Conversely, some very hardy shrubs, such as cotoneaster, are perfect for training against north-facing walls, where little else will grow. Other good flowering shrubs to train this way include: camellias, choisyas, daphnes, winter jasmine (*Jasminum nudiflorum*), pineapple broom (*Cytisus battandieri*), *Garrya elliptica* 'James Roof', and the mock orange *Philadelphus* 'Manteau d'Hermine'.

Ground cover

The job of providing effective ground cover falls to those plants that are able to cover the soil with a continuous canopy of attractive, preferably evergreen, foliage, which can suppress weeds. Ideally, it should be low-growing, quick-spreading and non-invasive.

A few flowering shrubs make good ground cover under trees and around other shrubs. However, most take time to establish a continuous blanket of interest. That blanket can be at least knee-deep in some cases, so bear this in mind when making your choice. Most ground-cover shrubs are pretty robust and don't mind if you walk on them if you need to.

To avoid detracting from the existing display, plant plain green ground cover beneath variegated shrubs. Under deciduous shrubs, evergreen ground-cover shrubs would extend the period of interest over winter. Try *Berberis thunbergii* f. *atropurpurea* 'Atropurpurea Nana',

A planting of tree-like magnolias has been used to create a mini-woodland effect at the bottom of this suburban garden.

wintergreen (*Gaultheria procumbens*) and the periwinkles (*Vinca*).

Growing shrubs over bare ground can also be a clever way of covering an awkward slope or bank. The shrubs will help to bind the soil together and blanket the soil with foliage, and so prevent weeds from growing up. Over sunny banks try *Santolina chamaecyparissus* 'Nana', *Ceanothus griseus* var. *horizontalis* 'Yankee Point' or *Genista lydia*. (*See also* page 110.)

Rock gardens

Some dwarf flowering shrubs are suitable for growing in a rockery, but make sure that you choose slow-growing plants that aren't invasive either above or below ground. *Berberis thunbergii* f. *atropurpurea* 'Atropurpurea Nana', for example, is ideal, reaching just 60cm (2ft) high when fully grown. In early spring it's smothered in pale yellow, red-tinged flowers, while its dense foliage turns fiery shades in autumn. Similarly, the cream-coloured deciduous broom *Cytisus* × *kewensis* reaches just 30cm (12in) high, although it may need pruning to restrict its spread. If you want an evergreen, *Hebe pinguifolia* 'Pagei' is a good choice. It has bluish-green foliage that looks good all year. Where space is at a premium, use the compact-growing heathers or heaths, such as *Calluna vulgaris* 'Dark Star' and *Erica carnea* 'Myretoun Ruby' or 'Springwood White'.

Centrepieces and mini-woodlands

Many people would like to include a tree or several trees in the garden but lack the space to do so. However, bear in mind that there are many flowering shrubs that can create very similar effects. They can be used either on their own, as a focal point, or may be grouped to create an intimate woodland effect, underplanted with a mixed planting of shade-tolerant bulbs, perennials and compact flowering shrubs. For more ideas on using tree-like shrubs, *see* pages 26–7.

Shrubs for wildlife

Many flowering shrubs provide the perfect environment for birds, insects and other creatures to set up home in your garden. They also produce fruits and flowers, which provide vital food sources throughout the seasons. With the decline in the bumblebee population, and the serious implications this has for the pollination of our food plants, we should all be doing our bit to attract pollinating insects to our gardens. To achieve this, include a mixture of both deciduous and evergreen flowering shrubs.

Bees and butterflies love the nectar-rich flowers of buddleia. This large shrub grows well at the back of sunny borders.

Attracting bees

Bees are looking for nectar and pollen. They are especially attracted to blue, purple, violet and yellow flowers, and are drawn to white and other colours if the fragrance is strong. Aim for a succession of flowers through the growing season, and bear in mind that single, rather than double, flowers offer easier access to the pollen and nectar. Bees appreciate a water source – a bowl of water, with a few pebbles for them to rest on, is adequate. Encourage bees to nest by providing short lengths of hollow cane. Bees' favourite shrubs include: berberis, buddleia, Mexican orange blossom (*Choisya*), sun rose (*Cistus*), cotoneaster, escallonia, rock rose (*Helianthemum*), *Lonicera × purpusii*, lavender, perovskia, potentilla, heathers, pyracantha, flowering currant (*Ribes*), rosemary, sage and thyme.

Attracting birds

Resident songbirds will eat berries during the autumn to help build up their reserves for winter. Try to include a range of flowering shrubs, such as berberis, cotoneaster and viburnum, which will not only look good but will provide food throughout the autumn and into winter, too. Bear in mind that a few berry-producing shrubs, including *Skimmia japonica*, need both male and female plants to be in the vicinity for the female plants to bear a good crop of fruit each year.

Some easy-to-grow shrubs produce an abundance of flowers in spring, followed by berries in autumn. Both are good for wildlife.
① *Viburnum opulus* 'Compactum' berries.
② The flowers of *Berberis darwinii*.

Ten ways to be a wildlife-friendly gardener

■ Grow a wide range of different shrubs that provide nectar and berries. A combination of these will provide food for insects (including bees and butterflies) and birds.

■ Your garden should consist of a good balance of grass (long and short if possible), trees, shrubs, flowers and water. Each of these provides a habitat for wildlife.

■ Provide a mixture of vegetation, light, shade and shelter for maximum diversity.

■ Include a mixture of early- and late-flowering plants. These will provide nectar for insects at critical times – just after emergence or prior to hibernation.

■ Leave tidying of borders and shrubs until late winter or early spring. This will provide shelter for insects and will retain seeds and fruits for birds and small mammals to feed on throughout winter.

■ A thorny shrub bed or hedge provides a vital nesting site as well as shelter for wildlife (berberis is particularly good for this).

■ Grow climbers against walls to provide shelter, and roosting and breeding sites, for birds.

■ Create a water feature, such as a pond – as well as attracting amphibians, water encourages birds and insects to the garden to drink and bathe.

■ Plant a wildlife garden and include native plants such as hawthorn (*Crataegus*).

■ Provide nesting boxes, bird baths and bird feeders to attract birds to the garden. Ensure they are safe from cats, squirrels and other animals.

In late summer, hungry birds won't be able to make the distinction between your fruiting shrubs and your crops on any nearby soft-fruit bushes, so if you grow raspberries and other soft fruits for a late-summer harvest, you should protect them with a fruit cage covered with netting.

To attract seed-eating birds such as goldfinches, plant a few sunflowers at the back of a shrub border, so that they can feast on the ripe seedheads towards the end of the year. Put food out regularly throughout the winter months, stopping during late spring to encourage the birds to forage for garden pests instead. Also, put up nesting boxes to suit a range of different birds, securing them to a wall, fence or tree at the back of a border, in order to provide the ideal cover. *See also* Plants for a purpose, page 44, for a selection of flowering shrubs that produce berries.

Attracting butterflies

To attract adult butterflies to your garden, include some nectar-rich flowering shrubs. There is the aptly named butterfly bush (*Buddleja*), but escallonia, hebe, lavender, lilac and thyme will also do the job. You can further encourage butterflies to visit your garden from mid-spring to late autumn by planting other nectar-rich flowering plants in and around your

shrubs. To lure the native early-spring butterflies, such as orange-tips, as well as the overwintering adults of small tortoiseshell and peacock butterflies, underplant with forget-me-nots, polyanthus and wallflowers. The flowering shrubs will then come into their own, but could be supplemented with a scattering of candytuft, helichrysum, heliotrope and lobelia. You will attract not only the native butterflies, but also summer visitors,

Planting long drifts of nectar-rich shrubs and herbs will draw butterflies and bees to your garden.
① *Hebe* 'Watson's Pink'.
② *Thymus* Coccineus Group.
③ *Lavandula angustifolia* 'Hidcote'.

such as the painted lady. By late summer, the butterfly bush will be a throng of busy insects. *Escallonia rubra* var. *macrantha* and *Cerastostigma willmottianum* will continue the rich nectar supply for the insects into the autumn months.

Shrubs in tubs

Many flowering shrubs are ideal for growing in pots. They make long-lasting container plants that can be used to transform a patio or fill gaps in borders. Shrubs in tubs can be used as flowering focal points and can be moved into prominent positions when they're looking their best. Matching containers planted with identical flowering shrubs can be used to provide a visual link between disparate elements of the garden – leading the casual visitor on to explore further.

If you don't have acid soil, you can grow azaleas such as *Rhododendron* 'Geisha Red' in containers.

The benefits

There are many advantages to growing flowering shrubs in containers. For example, it enables you to grow shrubs that would otherwise struggle to thrive in your existing soil. If you have chalky soil that is too alkaline to grow acid-lovers, such as pieris, camellias and rhododendrons, you can grow them in tubs filled with ericaceous compost. If your garden soil is heavy clay or waterlogged, you can still grow silver-leaved flowering shrubs that need dry soil, such as lavender, in pots filled with free-draining compost. Plus, borderline-hardy flowering shrubs planted in tubs can be grown outdoors in places where they would normally be killed off in winter by frost. All you need to do is move the container-grown specimen into a sheltered spot for the winter months, so that it's protected from the worst of the winter weather. You can even grow tender shrubs in tubs outside, provided you have somewhere frost free, such as a greenhouse, conservatory or light-filled porch, to keep them throughout the colder months.

Choosing shrubs

Which flowering shrub you select to grow in a container is very much a matter of personal choice, but bear in mind a few considerations.

First, think about where the container will be positioned – you will need to take note of how much sun it will get and how sheltered the site is. If the container is very large and heavy, it will probably stay in

Shrubs like white hydrangeas grow well in pots in dappled shade. Here, they brighten up a passage beneath a pergola covered in Virginia creeper.

the same spot once planted. Medium-sized or large tubs can be fitted with outdoor castors, or can be moved using a trolley or a special pot-moving platform.

A wide range of flowering shrubs can be grown in containers successfully, but the best long-term residents include azaleas, camellias, choisyas, hebes, pieris, dwarf rhododendrons, *Skimmia japonica* and *Viburnum davidii*. They must all be able to tolerate a restricted root-run and drought. Ideally, they should have an attractive outline and look good all year. Evergreens can often be planted as a single specimen, but deciduous shrubs will benefit from partners. You could try an underplanting of spring-flowering bulbs and a cascading evergreen edging plant, such as a small-leaved variegated ivy, to extend the period of interest.

Choosing containers

You can use almost any type of container, provided you select a suitable flowering shrub to match. Most will need as large a container as you can afford, ideally at least 45cm (18in) deep and wide, but there are flowering shrubs, including dwarf forms of hebe, that can be grown in much smaller containers.

Don't forget

Small flowering shrubs may need repotting into larger containers as they grow. Once the shrub is in its final container, skim off the top 5cm (2in) of compost each spring and replace it with fresh compost. Unless the plant is very slow-growing, it will eventually need moving out of its pot into the garden. Another option is to keep it artificially small by trimming back its roots each autumn.

Large shrubs in containers, such as this standard lilac (*Syringa meyeri* 'Palibin'), can be moved into place to add seasonal drama to a sunny patio.

Remember, terracotta pots dry out more quickly than glazed, stone or wooden ones, although you can line them with plastic to prevent drying out. Plastic pots tend to overheat in summer and don't provide sufficient insulation in winter for the roots of borderline-hardy shrubs; however, you can wrap them in bubble wrap for added protection. Avoid containers that narrow at the neck, as it will be hard to get a large shrub out without damaging the plant (or pot).

Planting and aftercare

When planting a shrub in a new container, cover the bottom of the pot with a layer of mesh then a 3cm (1¼in) layer of drainage material, such as stones or crocks, making the layer twice as deep for plants that like free-draining soil. Fill the pot with a loam-based compost such as John Innes No. 3, rather than a loamless compost, which will lose its structure with time. You can also mix in water-retaining granules, which will hold on to moisture. Covering the surface of the compost with stones will also help reduce water loss. (*See also* pages 52–3.)

Container-grown flowering shrubs need to be fed regularly in the growing season, either by watering with a liquid feed, or by inserting a slow-release fertilizer at planting time (and each spring thereafter). It is also a good idea to rotate permanent container plants once in a while, otherwise they turn towards the sun and grow unevenly.

Designing with flowering shrubs

Before planting a new border, you'll need to think about variety of shape, colour and texture, how each plant will fit into the whole, and the impact of the scheme at various times of the year. Flowering shrubs will be among the largest plants in a mixed border, so it's vital to consider their eventual height and width, and how the display will change over time as the plants develop. Some shrubs take off quickly, while others won't flower at their best until they start to mature a few years hence.

Where to start

One of the first things to think about when designing with shrubs is the depth of the borders. Bear in mind that you should normally allow about 1.5m (5ft) all round an average shrub that you might place at the back of the border. So in order to have a border containing a good mixture of shrubs of different shapes and sizes, you need to make it a minimum of 2.5m (8ft) deep. This will allow room for the three levels of planting that you'll find in all successful borders – at the front, below eye level; in the middle, at eye level; and at the back of the border, above eye level (*see* page 11).

The garden will be very much more interesting if you create borders of different depths, the minimum being 1m (40in). And any professional garden designer will tell you never to have beds running parallel to the edges of a rectangular or square plot.

As a rule of thumb, you should aim for about one third of your garden to be flower borders, and two thirds to be 'space' – that is, grass, paving, gravel and the like. There are exceptions to every rule, of course, but in most cases this will be about the right proportion.

Creating a border

The first step is to draw up your garden design on paper, then mark out the borders on the ground. Do this either with trails of sand poured from a plastic bottle or with a hosepipe warmed with water to make it more flexible. This will help you to visualize what your garden will look like. In your mind's eye, imagine those borders filled with plants.

Once you're happy with the size and shape of the beds, go back to the paper plan and mark out areas of shadow at different times of the day (and, ideally, at different times of the year, but you can only do this if you've had the garden for at least

Long-flowering shrubs, such as hebes, hydrangeas and roses, provide a lavish, summer-long display as well as giving structure to a border design.

a year). This is so you can see which areas are in permanent shade, temporary shade or permanent sunshine. Apart from helping you to decide where you might want to position any seating, this will enable you to select shrubs that will do well in each of these areas.

Remember, before you get down to choosing plants make sure you know your soil type to avoid making costly mistakes (*see* pages 48–9).

Casting the principal players

If you find the design process a bit daunting, you might find it helpful to think of flowering shrubs as the main characters in a play and the border as their stage. As the play unfolds, the main characters might take on different costumes (flowers, leaf colour and fruits), while the supporting cast (of perennials, climbers and bulbs) complement them and help to complete the

Dramatic when in bloom during late summer, the evergreen *Itea ilicifolia* makes a handsome foil for neighbouring plants at other times.

performance. Some flowering shrubs are so bold and imposing they should be considered the 'stars' of the show.

Choose flowering shrubs with different heights, so that you can maintain interest at every level. Large shrubs are obvious candidates for the back of deep borders. That way, they do not block the view of other, smaller plants. The height of background shrubs should depend on the depth of the border, so for a border 2.5–3m (8–10ft) deep, you could select shrubs with an ultimate height of 2.5–3m (8–10ft), whereas if the border were 5m (16ft) deep, shrubs with an ultimate height of

5m (16ft) would produce a more balanced result. If you wanted to include a particularly large shrub in the design, position it in a corner so that it doesn't dominate the rest of the planting scheme.

When thinking about plants for the middle and front of the border, it's easiest to plan them in several small groups. Within each group try to include a variety of shapes, colours – both flower and foliage – and textures. Ideally, intersperse vividly contrasting groups with quieter, more calming combinations. For more on the use of colour *see* pages 28–35. Don't forget to include a few shrubs selected for fragrance.

See pages 40–2 for examples of successful border plans. *See also* Plants for a purpose, pages 43–5, for ideas for flowering shrubs to use for different purposes and effects.

Some shrubs, like this spring-flowering *Magnolia × soulangeana* 'Lennei', make stunning specimens that draw the eye like a magnet when in bloom.

Which of us hasn't leaned into the flowers of a mock orange bush to breathe that fragrance in deep? Or rubbed a sprig of lavender through our fingers as we pass by? Or been stopped in our tracks by the heady scent of a daphne on a wintry morning? Fragrance is one of the greatest pleasures a garden can give. Yet it can be frustratingly elusive.

Scent is a highly subjective matter. Each of us perceives fragrance in a different way, and not all of us can smell all scents. So while one of us just loves the smell of lilac (*Syringa*), another will not. Some people adore the spicy smell of wintersweet (*Chimonanthus praecox*), but find the heady winter fragrance of *Daphne bholua* 'Jacqueline Postill' totally repellent. And you have to add into the equation the fact that smell, more than any other sense, can elicit an emotional response, evoking

You can enjoy fragrance in the garden all year round if you choose the right shrubs. ①An enclosed seating area is the best place to enjoy the heady scents of honeysuckle and lavender in summer. ② The flowers of *Osmanthus delavayi* 'Pearly Gates' are exquisitely fragrant in spring.

memories that influence our like or dislike of any given scent.

So when it comes to choosing plants to create that fragrant garden of your dreams, you simply have to seek out the ones that appeal to your individual taste. Plants to consider for borders near a seating or dining area include abelia, buddleia, Mexican orange blossom (*Choisya*), viburnum, osmanthus, broom (*Cytisus*), lavender and other aromatics such as rosemary. Winter-flowering shrubs have especially strong scents: put a daphne, Christmas box (*Sarcococca confusa*), honeysuckle (*Lonicera × purpusii*), skimmia or witch hazel (*Hamamelis*) by a much-used path or doorway so you can enjoy it as you come and go. (*See also* page 44.)

Aromatic foliage

Several flowering shrubs, including cotton lavender (*Santolina*), lavender (*Lavandula*), myrtle (*Myrtus*), Russian sage (*Perovskia*), rosemary and thyme, have aromatic leaves that release their fragrance when lightly rubbed. The best place to plant flowering shrubs with aromatic foliage is close to a path or seating area in full sun. Ground-hugging thymes can be planted in cracks between paving so that they're lightly crushed underfoot, releasing their fragrance each time you walk by. Light rain can also bring out the fragrance of some shrubs.

Structure and form

When planning your garden borders, make sure you give some thought to structure and form as well as colour – they are just as important. A planting scheme that is immediately pleasing to the eye will be made up of carefully juxtaposed, contrasting shapes.

From a distance, the first thing you'll notice about shrubs is their overall 'outline' – their habit, height and scale – but look more closely and you'll see an incredible diversity of flower and leaf shapes as well.

Flower shapes

Shrubs produce flowers in an infinite variety of shapes and sizes, ranging from flat and open to long and elegant, forming a bell, tunnel or trumpet. Some flowering shrubs produce huge individual flowers, like the blowsy, plate-sized flowers of the tree peony *Paeonia suffruticosa* or the conspicuous, goblet-like blooms of *Magnolia × soulangeana*; others, such as ceanothus and spiraea, make up for their smaller-sized flowers by producing them in abundance.

How the flowers are carried on the plant also affects the overall look of the shrub. Some are erect and spiky, pointing to the sky, while others are pendulous, bowing modestly. They can be produced as solitary blooms on separate stalks, or grouped in extravagant sprays or dense clusters. Flowers may be produced at the tips of shoots, or they may emerge from stubby spurs or from leaf-joints along the stems.

While many flowers offer only a fleeting display, several shrubs are renowned for blooming for months on end. These include *Hypericum* 'Hidcote', *Ceanothus × delileanus* 'Gloire de Versailles', *Potentilla fruticosa* 'Elizabeth' and *Viburnum tinus* 'Eve Price'. Mexican orange blossom (*Choisya*) will flower more than once, with the main display in late spring or early summer and a second flush in late summer or early autumn. For winter interest, opt for *Prunus incisa*, *Jasminum nudiflorum* and *Viburnum × bodnantense* 'Charles Lamont', which produce blooms on bare stems.

Leaf shapes

The leaf cover that shrubs provide is perhaps the most under-appreciated feature of flowering shrubs, but is absolutely key to the success of the design. Foliage fills out borders and gives schemes depth and structure.

Flowers come in a variety of shapes and sizes: the single, cup-shaped blooms of *Camellia sasanqua* 'Narumigata'; the conical clusters of tiny flowers produced by the yellow-orange *Buddleja × weyeriana* 'Golden Glow'; and the loose spikes of nodding, tubular flowers borne by *Phygelius aequalis* 'Yellow Trumpet'.

Diervilla × splendens has distinctive, puckered, purple-tinged green leaves that set off its clusters of sulphur-yellow flowers a treat.

Don't forget

It is vital to know where and on which type of growth a shrub bears its flowers, so that you can prune it correctly and encourage it to produce the best possible flowering displays (see pages 60–6).

Make the most of the vigorous, upright habit of the evergreen *Escallonia bifida* by growing it against a wall, where it will appreciate the extra protection.

with big, bold foliage, like *Fatsia japonica*, will jump forward. Similarly, blue-leaved plants tend to melt into the background, while flowering shrubs with brightly coloured foliage, like the golden-leaved mock orange *Philadelphus coronarius* 'Aureus', do the opposite.

Choosing shrub shapes

Flowering shrubs vary greatly in their outline. Some are shaggy, unkempt characters while others are neat and well groomed. Perhaps the most important consideration when selecting shrubs by their shape is their overall outline. As a rule, a border that contains several different shapes will work well as a whole.

Upright, fountain-shaped shrubs have a small 'footprint' in relation to their height, and so take up relatively little garden space. They offer dramatic, thrusting lines that can bring a design to life. Most fountain-shaped shrubs are naturally graceful and often look best when surrounded by low-growing plants or, if they are very large, when used to add drama to the back of a border. Good examples include:

Don't forget

Size and scale are important factors that contribute to the success of an architectural flowering shrub. It should not stick out like a sore thumb, or look like an awkward after-thought. Also bear in mind what the plant will look like when it is not in flower.

In the case of deciduous flowering shrubs, the foliage contribution is restricted to the spring, summer and autumn, but often with striking variations that add real interest when the garden is most used. The emerging new growth on some deciduous shrubs, including pieris, is as eye-catching as any flower, while shrubs like witch hazel (*Hamamelis*) and *Viburnum opulus* 'Compactum' develop such intense autumn tints that they become a beacon of colour at that time of the year. Deciduous shrubs with brightly coloured foliage, such as the purple-leaved *Berberis thunbergii* f. *atropurpurea* or the golden *Choisya ternata*

'Sundance', as well as those with variegated foliage, for example *Spiraea japonica* 'Anthony Waterer', will have a strong border presence throughout the growing season.

Evergreens go one step further, of course, offering continuity and structure throughout the year. That's not to say that they remain the same all year round – some, including many heathers, take on winter tints that dramatically alter their look.

Shrub foliage can also be used to alter the sense of perspective in a design. Fine-textured plants and those with tiny leaves, such as berberis and some hebes, will seem to recede from view, while those

Kolkwitzia amabilis 'Pink Cloud', *Kerria japonica*, *Berberis stenophylla*, *Deutzia* × *hybrida* 'Strawberry Fields', *Philadelphus* 'Belle Etoile' and *Viburnum* × *bodnantense* 'Dawn'.

Compact, dome-shaped flowering shrubs with a densely bushy habit include hebes, lavenders, santolinas and some potentilla varieties. However, you may have to prune them annually, in order to achieve the neatest outlines. Full, rounded shapes like this give the design body and a sense of permanence, which can be all year round if the plants are evergreen.

Low-spreading flowering shrubs, such as periwinkle (*Vinca*), can be used to cover the ground and fill gaps under taller shrubs and trees, as they are tolerant of shade, while sun-loving rock roses (*Helianthemum*) and thymes are useful on a sunny bank. In terms of their contribution towards the design, their low, spreading habit will emphasize the feeling of space in a border, because it leads the eye on a horizontal plane.

Using architectural forms

'Architectural' plants have one thing in common; a specific and highly prominent feature that cries out for attention. This can be their unusual shape – think mahonias or the contorted hazel; their larger-than-life presence – think *Fatsia japonica*; or a single dramatic feature, like the flowers of rhododendrons.

Architectural shrubs will always have border presence. Ensuring that they contrast with their surroundings, especially their background, is key in this. Some architectural plants are worth

With their architectural form and evergreen leaves, mahonias (here, *Mahonia* × *media*) have a dramatic impact on the garden throughout the year, but in late autumn and winter they stand like guardsmen, topped by a quiff of yellow flowers.

putting in a prominent position so they can be seen from more than one angle. This is easy when it's a stunning magnolia planted in a large lawn. An alternative would be a corner where two borders meet. Or, in a straight border you can realize this by bringing the shrub forwards, towards the front edge – this way it will stand out against the lower-growing plants on all sides.

Architectural plants do need to be handled with care, because if planted in the wrong place they could dominate their surroundings and upset the natural balance of the garden design as a whole.

The nearly shrubs

Some species classified as flowering shrubs are easy to confuse with perennials because their stems are woody only at the very base; this means they don't provide year-round structure as other shrubs do. They are often treated as herbaceous perennials, interspersed among other shrubs in a mixed border. Sometimes referred to as sub-shrubs, they include:

Bush clover (*Lespedeza thunbergii*), tree lupin (*Lupinus arboreus*), Russian sage (*Perovskia* 'Blue Spire'), tree poppy (*Romneya coulteri*), greater periwinkle (*Vinca major*) and lesser periwinkle (*Vinca minor; see* right).

There are many tall-growing shrubs that can be trained to form tree-like silhouettes; this is a useful way to add height to a garden design that is too small for real trees. Some large, tree-like shrubs, such as lilacs (*Syringa*) and magnolia, naturally shed their lower branches as they mature, while others can be trained like this. Larger flowering shrubs can also be useful for screening out unattractive views or for helping to increase a sense of privacy. Bear in mind that the closer you plant the shrubs to your vantage point, the smaller they have to be to form an effective screen.

Tree-like shrubs

Acacia dealbata
Amelanchier lamarckii
Aralia elata
Arbutus unedo
Azara dentata
Cercis siliquastrum
Clerodendrum trichotomum var. fargesii
Colutea arborescens
Cornus 'Eddie's White Wonder'
Cornus kousa var. chinensis
Cornus mas
Corylus avellana 'Contorta'
Cotinus coggygria 'Royal Purple'
Cotoneaster × watereri 'John Waterer'
Cytisus battandieri
Drimys winteri
Embothrium coccineum
Enkianthus campanulatus
Eucryphia × nymansensis 'Nymansay'
Halesia carolina
Leptospermum scoparium 'Red Damask'
Magnolia × loebneri 'Leonard Messel'
Magnolia × soulangeana
Olearia macrodonta
Pittosporum tobira
Prunus incisa
Prunus triloba
Syringa pubescens subsp. microphylla 'Superba'
Syringa vulgaris varieties
Tamarix ramosissima 'Pink Cascade'

There are tree-like shrubs for almost every situation, with examples that flower in every season. Many lilacs can be trained into tree-like shrubs, but varieties of common lilac (*Syringa vulgaris*) are probably the best. Try to choose a named variety, because species lilacs can make straggly and suckering, short-flowering specimens that have little garden value. Slightly more compact, *Syringa pubescens* subsp. *microphylla* 'Superba' is also worth considering for its superbly fragrant, conical clusters of rose-pink flowers, produced in late spring and then on and off until autumn. Both can be cut back to a knee-high stubby framework if they get too big, although you'll miss out on flowers for a few years. (For more recommended lilacs, see pages 104–5.)

There are tree-like shrubs for all gardens. ① *Eucryphia* × *nymansensis* 'Nymansay' reaches a height of about 15m (49ft). ② *Prunus triloba* (flowering almond) can reach 3m (10ft) tall.

Flowering focal points

If you want an evergreen multi-stemmed, tree-like shrub, consider the strawberry tree (*Arbutus unedo*), which will eventually reach 8m (26ft). A tall specimen is the best way to show off its attractive, shredding brown bark. The strawberry tree also bears clusters of white or pink-tinged flowers in autumn, at the same time as spherical fruits that ripen to red. The New Zealand tea tree *Leptospermum scoparium* 'Red Damask' will also make an elegant specimen, with arching

stems and double, deep-red flowers, produced *en masse* during late spring and early summer. It is ideal for growing at the back of a border, but in the UK will thrive only in mild, sheltered gardens.

For a deciduous tree-like shrub, choose either the Japanese angelica tree (*Aralia elata*), 10m (33ft) high, with its large sprays of small, white flowers during late summer and early autumn,

or the Judas tree (*Cercis siliquastrum*), which makes an excellent multi-stemmed specimen for a small garden. It becomes the centre of attention as its leaves emerge in spring, when the bare stems, branches, and even the trunk are covered in sugar-pink to near-purple flowers.

Flowering dogwoods, such as *Cornus* 'Eddie's White Wonder' or *Cornus kousa* var. *chinensis*, are always eye-catching with their creamy-white flower bracts and attractive foliage that turns fiery shades in autumn. Both eventually reach around 6–7m (20–23ft). For

winter colour in a small garden, the 5m (16ft) high cornelian cherry (*Cornus mas*) is a good option. It has frothy clusters of tiny, acid-yellow flowers, which stand out from bare branches during late winter, and the added bonus of cherry-red fruits towards the end of the following summer.

In a colder garden, try the silver bell *Halesia carolina*, which reaches 12m (39ft) high, becoming a mass of hanging snowdrop-like flowers, followed by winged, pear-shaped fruits. These make excellent specimen plants, but can take a few years to settle in before they flower. Alternatively, you could train a magnolia, perhaps *Magnolia × loebneri* 'Leonard Messel', which reaches 8m (26ft) and bears beautiful long-petalled, lilac-pink, star-shaped flowers on bare branches.

Don't forget

You can create a multi-stemmed specimen out of an existing upright, woody shrub in your garden by carrying out a bit of judicious pruning. Select the most vigorous stems and prune out all the others. Then cut off the lowest branches to reveal these main stems.

Flowering tree-like shrubs will create a dramatic seasonal point of focus.
① Judas tree (*Cercis siliquastrum*), a striking shrub, will grow to 10m (33ft) tall.
② Chinese dogwood (*Cornus kousa* var. *chinensis*) grows to 7m (23ft) tall.
③ Common lilac (*Syringa vulgaris*) reaches 7m (23ft) in height at maturity.

Combining colours

Colour brings out an emotional response, so finding the right flower, foliage and fruit colours for your garden can be a very personal quest. Colour also provides subconscious cues to mood and atmosphere, and it's an indication of the season, too. When designing a shrub border, it does not always pay to select old favourites without further thought. Instead, it's wiser to choose colours that work together.

Working with colour

The colour of plants has an impact on how you see a garden. Bright colours such as yellows, oranges and scarlet dominate, while blues, greens and silvery greys are 'quieter'. In between, pastel pinks and other pale shades jostle for attention.

You can use this knowledge to your advantage when designing a planting scheme. For example, you can increase the sense of space, making a garden seem longer and wider than it really is, by planting the dominant colours near points from which you will be viewing the garden, such as the house and the patio, and using the recessive colours at the edges and the bottom of the garden. Conversely, in a large garden, you can manipulate colours in order to create the illusion of intimacy and seclusion.

This effect can be reinforced by the choice of foliage. Large-leaved plants, especially those with a glossy green sheen, and plants with a clear outline, will seem closer than they really are, while ferny and filigree foliage plants will melt into the background, increasing the sense of space and distance.

Combining colours is not straightforward, because how we see a particular border scheme is influenced by personal preference, light levels – including the time of day – and the setting. Each colour has its own character and complexity, and this affects how it reacts with its neighbours and how it influences the scheme as a whole. A further complication is that the flowers of shrubs are not one single pure colour, but a blend of hues.

Hydrangeas display their glorious range of blue and mauve shades to enhance the intimacy and restful mood of a secluded wooded glade.

Late summer blooming plumbago, *Ceratostigma willmottianum* 'Forest Blue', is covered in clusters of vivid pale blue flowers.

True-blue California lilacs, such as *Ceanothus arboreus* 'Trewithen Blue', will produce a profusion of minute fragrant flowers from late spring.

Ground-hugging *Lithodora diffusa* 'Heavenly Blue' bears deep azure-blue flowers in profusion from late summer into autumn.

Blue

Cool and calming, blue is one of the most restful colours in the spectrum and contributes a soothing and contemplative air to a planting scheme. It is a very recessive colour, too, and visually brings a sense of space into a flower border and garden design. This can be particularly useful when working with small gardens.

Blue is also a wonderfully accommodating colour. Like green and white, which are the other cool hues, blues can be combined effectively with almost any other colour. Blue flowers make the perfect chaperone for other more dramatic blooms – their understated dignity increasing the vibrancy of more spectacular bedfellows. They work well with yellow in spring schemes, with rich reds in early summer, and with contrasting colours, like lime green.

All-blue schemes can also be stunning; try combining deep and powdery shades, or purplish and soft-violet hues. Bear in mind, however, that our perception of blue changes as light levels increase or diminish. Above all, remember that the colour is at its best in dappled light, while in direct sunlight it can look purple.

Blue is perhaps the most elusive flower colour in the garden: rose breeders have tried for years to produce a true-blue rose, but without success. Several flowering shrubs have blue flowers, including caryopteris (clear blue), ceanothus (powder blue to deep blue), ceratostigma (rich blue), rosemary (purple-blue) and hibiscus (maroon-centred, violet-blue) – and even these vary markedly depending on variety. With some hydrangeas, the colour can be influenced by where they grow (*see* box, right).

Don't forget

Blue is calming, cool and luminous, and shows up well in shade and when light levels are low, at dawn and dusk. It combines well with other blues, whites and greens for harmonious results and offers a vivid contrast with orange.

Making hydrangeas blue

The flower colour of some common hydrangeas (*Hydrangea macrophylla*) is affected by the pH of the soil. In acid soils, with a pH of less than 5.5, they're blue. On soils with a higher pH, they often appear in various shades of pink. The reason for this is that in order to produce blue flowers, hydrangeas need to take up aluminium ions. Although most soils contain plenty of aluminium, hydrangeas can absorb sufficient amounts only if the soil is acidic.

If you don't have acidic soil, you can turn hydrangeas blue by watering the plant with a solution of sulphur or aluminium sulphate. However, these treatments won't work if your soil is very alkaline. In this case, to achieve true-blue hydrangeas you'll have to grow them in pots filled with ericaceous (preferably peat-free) compost. Always water hydrangeas with collected rainwater rather than tap water, particularly in hard-water areas.

Lilacs produce dense, conical spikes of fragrant flowers in a range of colours, including violet-blue, during late spring and early summer.

Erica × darleyensis 'Ghost Hills' produces spikes of flowers from midwinter, above mounds of cream-tipped, pale green foliage.

Graceful *Buddleja alternifolia* really enjoys the early-summer sun. At this time of the year, it will be festooned with fragrant flowers.

Violets and purples

Purples and violets are warmer than blues, with an underlying richness – indeed, they are often associated with the trappings of wealth and social importance. The darkest shades, as in the leaves of *Sambucus nigra* 'Eva', are the nearest plant colour to black and add a sense of brooding to a border. In shady sites, remember that purples appear darker and more moody.

Violets and purples are essentially cool and recessive. They mix well with greens and each other, but they're easily overwhelmed by stronger, brighter colours. Shy and introspective, they do not look great when dotted through a border. Instead, they should be planted in broad brush strokes, which is why flowering shrubs that produce large individual purple flowers, such as rhododendrons, or smaller blooms *en masse*, like buddleia, are the most effective. Other flowering shrubs

with varieties that have beautiful purple or violet flowers include hebe, lilac, lavender, magnolia, rosemary and thyme.

Purple comes into its own when mixed with a contrasting colour, for instance yellow or orange – you have only to think how striking this combination is in the orange-eyed, violet-blue flowers of *Buddleja* 'Lochinch'. The brilliant golden foliage of the mock orange *Philadelphus coronarius* 'Aureus' will make a striking partner for many shrubs with purple flowers. You could also experiment by blending purples with reds.

Alternatively, a splash of silver or grey will bring a deep purple to life. Try placing the fragrant, dark purple flowers of *Buddleja davidii* 'Black Knight' alongside the deep-purple spikes of *Lavandula angustifolia* 'Munstead', which are set off against the lavender's aromatic, grey-green leaves.

Don't forget

Shades of violet and purple recede into border plantings. Combine the lighter shades with pale pinks and blues for a soothing result and with dark violets, purples and magenta for drama. Purple contrasts with yellow.

Using purple foliage

Purple foliage is one of the best ways of bringing richness and interest to a planting scheme. Leaves vary from bronze-purple, through reddish purple, to almost black. Striking flowering shrubs with purple foliage include the plum-coloured smoke bush *Cotinus coggygria* 'Royal Purple' and the black elder *Sambucus nigra* 'Eva', which has deep-purple foliage that turns jet black when viewed in shade. Also spectacular are varieties of *Berberis thunbergii*, such as 'Dart's Red Lady' and the deep red-purple 'Bagatelle' and 'Helmond Pillar'. Other shrubs with dark foliage include: *Corylus maxima* 'Purpurea', *Physocarpus opulifolius* 'Diabolo' and *Viburnum sargentii* 'Onondaga'.

Purple-leaved flowering shrubs make excellent backdrops for other flowering plants with contrasting colour blooms. Orange tulips, such as the glowing orange-red 'World's Favourite' and the softer orange 'Ballerina', look wonderful with purple-leaved shrubs.

Stunning in flower, this New Zealand tea tree, *Leptospermum scoparium* 'Red Damask', will be aglow with blooms from late spring.

Flowers of *Magnolia × soulangeana* varieties are borne on bare stems and vary from white through every shade of pink to violet-purple.

Smothered in starry, candy-striped flowers from late spring, the compact *Deutzia × elegantissima* 'Rosealind' is ideal for small gardens.

Pink

A symbol of good health and romance, pink is a paler form of red (*see* page 35). Like reds, pinks can be broadly divided into two groups: the warmer peachy shades that are derived from the yellow hue found in 'hot reds', such as scarlet and vermilion; and the cooler shell pinks, which have a hint of blue and are based on crimson.

Working with pink

As a rule, 'warm' and 'cool' pinks do not sit happily together in a planting scheme. For a harmonious result, it's often best to put them with whites: warm pinks with creamy whites, and cool pinks with bluish whites. Also, despite its close relationship with red, pink does not make a good companion for strong reds such as scarlet and crimson, while saturated yellows and oranges do not seem to mix with any shade of pink at all.

In their paler form, cool shell pinks are calming and recessive. Think, for example, of the flowers of *Erica carnea* 'Challenger' or the purplish-pink blooms of *Daphne mezereum*. These beautiful, cool shades make lovely harmonious combinations with other cool colours including mauves, blues and the violet side of purple. Saturated magenta shades, however, demand attention. If you're brave enough, try the eye-watering combination of the cerise-pink French lavender *Lavandula stoechas* 'Kew Red', and deep-purple *Buddleja davidii* 'Black Knight'. In bright light, the more saturated pinks steal the show, but in half-light at dawn or dusk, and in the dappled light underneath trees, the pale shades come to the fore.

Think peaches and cream when it comes to warm pinks, which are generally easy on the eye – for example, the pale to deep-pink, bell-shaped flowers of *Kolkwitzia*

amabilis, or the pink-flushed white flowers of *Lavatera × clementii* 'Barnsley'. As warm pinks mellow, they turn apricot, as seen in the rock rose *Helianthemum* 'Amy Baring' and the flowering quince *Chaenomeles speciosa* 'Geisha Girl'.

An excellent shrub or small tree, *Cornus* 'Eddie's White Wonder' produces large white bracts that surround the tiny green flowers.

Ideal for lighting up dappled shade, *Viburnum* 'Eskimo' produces its snowball-shaped heads of pure white flowers from pink-tinted buds.

Upright branches of *Fabiana imbricata* carry masses of tubular, white flowers in plumes during early summer, if given full sun.

White

White flowering shrubs are great companion plants, and the garden designer's ally, because they look good with every other colour. A sign of purity and perfection, white is strong enough to use on its own, looking its sophisticated best in dappled shade or in the fading light at the end of the day. The classic all-white border can be found in the garden designs of many a stately home, but a pure white scheme is equally at home in a contemporary urban garden.

Brilliant whites shine out from a shady border like beacons from the gloom; they can give the whole border a 'lift'. Whites also do the job of increasing luminosity in shady sites, by reflecting light into the deepest recesses. Similarly, in sunny sites, white flowers and silver foliage can be a winning combination.

Of course, whites are sometimes trickier to use than they seem at first glance, with bluish whites and apple whites lending themselves to planting among cooler colours, especially, blues, mauves, shell pinks, crimson reds and purples. Ivory and creamy whites – with a hint of yellow in them – are more at home alongside warmer colours, such as scarlet reds, peachy pinks, and apricot shades. Also, many flowers that appear pure white are actually flecked and daubed with other colours; use these as a guide when choosing suitable colour companions. In fact, this can be a fail-safe way of putting together a successful colour scheme. Start with the white, match its partners to the subtle markings within its petals and your scheme will be halfway there, as each new plant chosen reinforces the colour of its neighbour.

An all-white scheme

For an all-white planting in dappled shade, try the creamy-white snowball clusters of *Hydrangea arborescens* 'Annabelle' with the weeping branches of *Exochorda* × *macrantha* 'The Bride' and *Philadelphus* 'Belle Etoile'; underplant this with white dicentra, phlox and towering foxgloves – it will look good in late spring and early summer. In a monochrome planting scheme, contrast in habit and foliage are particularly important.

Interestingly, white flowers tend to have the richest fragrance. This is because pollinating insects are often attracted to plants for their colour; because white flowers lack colour, they need to attract insects in other ways – hence their alluring scent.

Evergreen shrubs for year-round interest

Evergreen flowering shrubs are indispensable. Choose the right ones and, as well as a sense of permanence and structure in the display, you'll get a spectacular show of flowers that can transform the appearance of a whole garden.

If you have the space, you can get flowering evergreens to bloom every month of the year, providing a continuity of colour and interest. Although many evergreen shrubs are hardy, some are vulnerable to damage from cold winds that singe leaves and shoots and disfigure early flowers. In addition, in colder regions, you would be wise to protect any less-than-hardy evergreen flowering shrubs over the winter months (*see* page 59).

A year of colour

Spring-flowering evergreen shrubs are the most spellbinding, and easily rival the swathes of spring-flowering bulbs and massed bedding displays for colour at this time of year. Bear in mind that some spring-flowering evergreen shrubs, including azaleas, rhododendrons and camellias, need a lime-free soil to thrive. In a garden with chalky soil, however, they can be successfully grown in containers filled with ericaceous compost to create the right growing conditions. There are spring-flowering evergreens that will grow in most gardens, including the fabulously scented Mexican orange blossom (*Choisya*) or varieties of *Berberis* × *stenophylla* and *Berberis darwinii* for example, which make good informal boundary hedges and stunning medium-sized border shrubs for small and large gardens alike.

By summer, evergreens become important for providing a dark backdrop for other shrubs and plants that flower at this time of year. However, there are also a few choice flowering evergreens worth growing for their summer flowers, too. Escallonias and hebes make excellent informal, flowering hedges. Being tolerant of salt-laden winds, they are useful in coastal gardens in mild areas, where they can be used as windbreaks, sheltering smaller plants.

Among the best autumn-flowering evergreens are *Osmanthus heterophyllus*, which offers lovely, jasmine-scented, tubular flowers from late summer onwards, followed by oval, blue-black fruits. Or consider *Ceanothus* 'Autumnal Blue' or 'Burkwoodii', for their fluffy clusters of intensely blue flowers.

In winter, evergreens come into their own as their deciduous neighbours become stark and leafless. A few hardy souls will even blossom or fruit during the coldest months, making them doubly valuable. *Garrya elliptica* 'James Roof' will light up walls with its cloak of

Here are two favourite flowering shrubs for providing year-round interest.
① The lustrous foliage of *Choysia ternata* is the perfect foil for its fragrant, white, spring and late-summer/autumn flowers.
② Early sunlight catches the red-tinted flower buds of *Skimmia japonica* on a frosty winter's morning.

wavy-edged, green foliage, which sets off the tassel-like male catkins a treat. In the border, varieties of *Skimmia japonica* will produce tight clusters of red-tinted flower buds, which, on female or hermaphrodite plants, are followed by stunning crops of glossy red fruits.

The arching stems of *Cytisus × praecox* 'Allgold' are encrusted with deep-yellow, pea-like flowers. It will flower reliably in poor soils in sunny sites.

A mass of the orange-eyed, golden, cup-shaped flowers of *Helianthemum* 'Ben Fhada' will set the garden aglow in early summer.

Two-tone, apricot-yellow and red, bell-like flowers hang from the new shoots of *Abutilon* 'Kentish Belle' throughout the summer months.

Yellows and golds

Sunshine shades of yellow and gold are among the strongest colours in the spectrum, shouting out their presence in the border. Some people are not keen on yellow, and it can be difficult to use sucessfully with other colours as it can be too strong. But yellows are by nature warm and uplifting, and they can be used to great effect in planting schemes.

In most gardens, yellows and golds are perfect for dotting around the garden among larger blocks of other colours, adding sparkle to sombre foliage and a zest to dark colours. There are some useful flowering shrubs to help you achieve this effect. In addition, you could also consider shrubs with yellow foliage or fruit (*see* box, right).

Yellow is at its most attractive in spring, when the sun is less fierce. In fact, for many, this is the colour of the spring garden, with lemon-coloured daffodils and the brilliant *Forsythia × intermedia* 'Lynwood Variety' leading the way. You could start the display earlier by adding the primrose-yellow pendent flowers of *Corylopsis pauciflora*, or you could extend the show into early summer with the long-lasting, creamy-yellow blooms of *Cytisus × praecox* 'Warminster', and then on into late summer with the canary-yellow *Potentilla fruticosa* 'Elizabeth'.

Yellow hues range from the cooler, greenish, lemony shades of *Coronilla valentina* subsp. *glauca* 'Citrina' and *Cornus mas*, through to the bright, clear yellows of brooms (*Cytisus*). The winter jasmine (*Jasminum nudiflorum*) and *Fremontodendron* 'California Glory' also offer bright, clear shades, while scorching, orange-tinted, golden hues can be found in flowers of *Genista pilosa* 'Vancouver Gold', *Buddleja globosa* and many witch hazels (*Hamamelis*).

Adding more yellow

You can increase the impact of yellow flowers by including plants with other yellow features into your planting scheme, such as the fruits of flowering quince (*Chaenomeles*). A few flowering shrubs offer dramatic golden foliage, such as that of the mock orange *Philadelphus coronarius* 'Aureus' and the elder *Sambucus nigra* 'Aurea', or the bright yellow juvenile foliage of *Choisya ternata*. Other flowering shrubs have notable yellow-variegated forms, including *Abutilon megapotamicum*, *Aralia elata*, *Osmanthus heterophyllus*, *Viburnum tinus*, *Daphne odora*, as well as *Abelia × grandiflora* 'Francis Mason'.

Golden-yellow shades make bright, fiery combinations with reds and oranges, acid yellows work best with greens, while creamy yellows blend with dark pinks.

Small but perfectly formed, the burning orange-scarlet tubular flowers of *Fuchsia* 'Firecracker' are produced in abundance all summer.

Add real passion to your borders using flowering shrubs that bear blooms in flamboyant trusses, like this lipstick-red rhododendron.

Callistemon citrinus throws out a succession of crimson, bottlebrush-like flower spikes on arching stems in late spring and all summer.

Reds

Broadly speaking, red flowers can be divided into two camps: those that include a hint of yellow, like scarlet, and those that have blue tones in them, notably crimson. The former group are the 'hot reds' that appear like glowing embers in the garden – warm and inviting, drawing the eye. Hot reds mix well with other fiery colours, such as oranges and yellows, and can be used to really turn up the temperature. The 'moody reds', on the other hand, are cooler, slightly more recessive on the eye, and also more forgiving in combinations with other colours. The purple-reds are at the dark end of the moody-red spectrum, and they become more atmospheric and brooding as the light fades towards the end of the day. Deep plum and 'woodsmoke' reds are very recessive, and combine particularly well with bright greens.

When creating a hot border, you could mix flowering shrubs with tender and hardy perennials in hot red hues, as well as roses, to increase the number of flowers on show during the summer months. Use fully saturated scarlets and vermilions backed by blackish-red foliage, as in the *Dahlia* 'Bishop of Llandaff' or the black elder *Sambucus nigra* 'Eva', to create a harmonious yet brooding ambience. Extend the display into autumn with the plum-purple foliage of the smoke bush *Cotinus coggygria* 'Royal Purple', which turns fiery shades, or equally stunning climbers, such as Virginia creeper (*Parthenocissus quinquefolia*) or the crimson glory vine (*Vitis coignetiae*). Red and purple make an excellent atmospheric combination, but for a lighter feel, try the same vivid reds with fresh green foliage, for example, the summer-flowering *Potentilla* 'Gibson's Scarlet', the spring-blooming

Don't forget

Red is attention-grabbing and dramatic and is best seen at close range. Warm reds combine with oranges and yellows for vibrant effects; cool reds with dark blues, purples or golds for a sultry mood; and all reds contrast with green.

Incorporating orange

Brazen and attention-seeking, orange can be a difficult colour to incorporate into a planting scheme. In a summer border, you could try orange *Potentilla fruticosa* 'Tangerine' with the orange-centred, golden-yellow flowers of *Helianthemum* 'Ben Fhada'. Orange looks striking as a single colour with green, but it can also be blended with bronzes and browns for a more subdued display. In a small garden, orange is safer to use as 'spots' of colour rather than throughout a border. Plant up a pot with the azalea 'Gibraltar' or 'Klondyke', to provide a splash of spring colour on the terrace.

flowering currant *Ribes sanguineum* 'Pulborough Scarlet' or, for winter sparkle, the stunning crops of red fruits produced by the evergreen *Skimmia japonica* subsp. *reevesiana*.

Shrubs with other plants

Stalwarts of the mixed border, flowering shrubs can be combined successfully with almost any other type of plant. You can cover the ground under shrubs with ground-hugging perennials and bulbs, while taller perennials can be used to provide seasonal fireworks at the back of the border. Climbers, too, can be employed to scramble through established shrubs or trained to cover the bare ground beneath.

Good companions

Any plant that you grow underneath or through an established shrub will have to be able to put up with slightly difficult growing conditions. The soil under deciduous shrubs is usually drier than average, so choose shade-tolerant plants that are also drought-tolerant enough to cope.

It's also wise to consider how well the companion will complement the shrub that it is going to be teamed with. If they flower together, make sure the resulting display will be harmonious. You could also choose a plant that performs when the shrub is not in flower, so that you extend the season of interest.

Deciduous shrubs that leaf-up late in the spring will still offer light below their branches during early spring, and underplanted flowering bulbs will take advantage of this.

Underneath evergreen flowering shrubs, the shade will be deeper and might well be permanent, so you will have to choose really tough understorey plants that can tolerate low light levels if they're to survive. Planting on the south, east or west side of evergreens is the best idea, because then the plants underneath will get at least a bit of direct sun at some point during the day – either at the beginning or the end – when the sun is lower in the sky. Under large evergreen shrubs, another option might be to plant spreading species at the edge of the canopy and train them to cover the ground beneath the evergreen – this works well with some climbers, including many varieties of clematis, ivies and vines.

The fragrant, yellow-throated pink flowers of *Weigela praecox* are beautifully framed by the striking flower spikes of pink and yellow lupins.

An underplanting of bright blue, spring-flowering grape hyacinths here complements the metallic, holly-like foliage and acid-yellow flowers of *Mahonia aquifolium* 'Apollo'.

Underplanting bulbs

Although most bulbs need full sun to flower reliably year after year, many can still do well enough in dappled shade under deciduous flowering shrubs, for example elders (*Sambucus*) and hydrangeas. In a large shrub border, try planting bluebell bulbs, which will spread naturally over the years to form a rich carpet of blue every spring. You can even grow bluebells in a small garden if you dead-head them after flowering to prevent them from self-seeding, or you could try grape hyacinth (*Muscari*) instead. All gardens can accommodate dwarf narcissi, but these need some direct sunlight, either at the beginning or the end of the day. Good varieties include 'Hawera', 'Jack Snipe' and 'Tête-à-tête'. In light dappled shade, you could plant the more shade-tolerant bulbs, such as *Crocus tommasinianus*, *Cyclamen hederifolium* and *Cyclamen coum*, wood anemone (*Anemone nemorosa*), glory of the snow (*Chionodoxa forbesii*), dog's-tooth violet (*Erythronium*), winter aconite (*Eranthis hyemalis*), Siberian squill (*Scilla siberica*), snowdrops (*Galanthus nivalis*) or spring snowflake (*Leucojum vernum*). If you want to grow tender bulbs, which usually need lifting and storing each winter, provide protection by planting them among a low-growing shrub such as a periwinkle (*Vinca*).

All bulbs look best if scattered in random groups and planted where they land. When planting bulbs among the roots of established flowering shrubs, use a narrow trowel to open up individual planting holes, to avoid damaging the roots. Alternatively, create a special planting 'pocket' between the flowering shrubs. Fill the pocket with fresh topsoil augmented with well-rotted organic matter before planting the bulbs at random spacing to achieve a natural look.

Perennial ground cover

Many low-growing, shade-loving herbaceous perennials are ideal to plant as ground cover under flowering shrubs. This technique works particularly well in large borders and, once the ground is completely covered over, it will also keep down weeds. Many herbaceous perennials offer colourful foliage, as well as flowers. Some are evergreen and provide a year-round presence, which can be especially useful under deciduous flowering shrubs. For example, elephant's ears (*Bergenia cordifolia*), with its purple-tinted foliage and colourful spikes of early

This coordinated, late-spring display of rhododendron and weigela is complemented by the first bottlebrush-like spikes of *Persicaria bistorta*. This semi-evergreen perennial can tolerate the shady, dry soil conditions found around the shrubs, and makes an exceptionally long-flowering, ground-hugging plant.

flowers, will add winter interest right up until the deciduous flowering shrubs leaf-up in spring.

Try using contrasting foliage to provide added interest, too. For example, you could extend the display of evergreen shrubs such as rhododendrons and camellias, which flower for only a short period in spring, by planting lady's mantle

(*Alchemilla mollis*) around each of them – the ground cover will provide a striking frill of scalloped-shaped, lime-green leaves, topped by a frothy haze of yellow flowers all summer long.

You can supplement deciduous perennials that offer ground cover with an underplanting of bulbs, in order to extend their period of

Under the protection of eucalyptus, the frost-hardy, evergreen *Ceanothus* 'Skylark' is smothered in dark blue flowers in late spring.

reasonably well in dappled shade: rhododendrons (including azaleas), berberis, camellias, viburnums, pieris, mahonias, flowering quince (*Chaenomeles*), Mexican orange blossom (*Choisya*), *Fatsia japonica*, *Hypericum* 'Hidcote', *Osmanthus delavayi*, elder (*Sambucus*), Christmas box (*Sarcococca*), periwinkles (*Vinca*) and skimmias.

Scrambling climbers

In the wild, a climber will use flowering shrubs for support. In the garden, growing climbers up and through shrubs can be an excellent way of showing both of them off to best effect. The key is to choose the right climber, so that the host shrub does not become swamped. It is best to avoid using very vigorous climbers, such as varieties of *Clematis montana* and *Clematis tangutica*, ornamental creepers (*Vitis* or *Parthenocissus*) or the Russian vine (*Fallopia baldschuanica*). Large, tree-like shrubs such as magnolias, philadelphus and lilacs make excellent host plants and can cope with fairly vigorous climbers. For example, an early to midsummer flowering mock orange, such as *Philadelphus* 'Manteau d'Hermine', could be teamed with a variety of

interest. They work well together, as the emerging foliage on the perennials in spring will help to disguise the fading, yellowing leaves of the spring-flowering bulbs.

When planting ground cover, you can use just one species throughout or create a tapestry effect using a mix of species – these work best when you plant in groups of odd numbers, using at least three plants. Your planting scheme can be formal or informal, to suit the rest of the garden. If your aim is to suppress the growth of weeds, first you will have to remove all existing weeds from the area, including the roots of perennials, and then continue weeding through the growing season until the ground cover forms a complete carpet. The best

perennials for covering the ground in shade include bugles (*Ajuga*), elephant's ears (*Bergenia*), lily-of-the-valley (*Convallaria*), hostas, *Lamium*, hellebores, *Pulmonaria* and *Tiarella*, but you could also try some of the lovely ornamental grasses available, such as *Miscanthus* and *Stipa*.

Under trees

A few shade-tolerant flowering shrubs are suitable for planting under trees that have an open canopy – such as silver birch, laburnum, ash, rowan and fruit trees. Large-leaved trees, such as sycamore, and others that produce a dense canopy, like beech, are less suitable because not enough light will filter through. However, any of the following shrubs will flower

Don't forget

For a quick and cheap ground-cover solution, plant bedding plants and annuals between flowering shrubs. These will last for a single season. For filling gaps between shrubs that get at least some direct sun, you could try love-lies-bleeding (*Amaranthus caudatus*), *Cosmos bipinnatus*, pot marigold (*Calendula officinalis*) or forget-me-not (*Myosotis*). Pot marigolds and forget-me-nots will happily self-seed and naturalize, and will therefore reappear year after year.

Clematis macropetala is a fabulous choice for growing through a shrub (here, hibiscus). It flowers from late spring through to early summer.

Climbers to grow through shrubs

Akebia quinata

Clematis (large-flowered hybrids , for example 'Ernest Markham', 'Nelly Moser', Perle d'Azur', 'The President' and 'Ville de Lyon')

Clematis alpina

Clematis flammula

Clematis macropetala

Humulus lupulus 'Aureus'

Lathyrus latifolius

Trachelospermum

Tropaeolum

alpine clematis (*Clematis alpina*), which would flower in spring and produce attractive, fluffy seedheads during autumn, effectively spreading the period of interest over three seasons. Similarly, you could pair a late summer flowering everlasting pea (*Lathyrus latifolius*) with a spring-flowering magnolia to double its garden value. For a colour contrast, try the vine-like leaves of golden hop (*Humulus lupulus* 'Aureus') trained through the purple-black foliage of the elder *Sambucus nigra* 'Gerda' (formerly f. *porphyrophylla* 'Black Beauty').

Many climbers are as happy scrambling across the ground as they are growing up a support. They make interesting and unusual ground cover between permanent flowering shrubs, and they produce such long, trailing stems that they are able to cover ground where little else will grow, even in the dense, dry shade found under evergreens. Choose shade-lovers such as ivies and Virginia creeper (*Parthenocissus quinquefolia*) for these sites; but for light, dappled shade or areas of temporary shade, your choice of climbers increases to include clematis and honeysuckles. For something more unusual, try the chocolate vine (*Akebia*), *Ampelopsis* or *Trachelospermum*.

Planning a border

Putting flowering shrubs with other plants to make a border that really works can be a challenge to both your artistic talent and your problem-solving skills. The plants must look good together, of course, and this means thinking about seasons as well as shape, structure and colour. But if the plants are to give of their best, they must also be right for the soil, aspect and climate of the chosen site.

Multi-tasking shrubs

Some of the showiest and best-known flowering shrubs can be quite difficult to integrate into mixed borders. Large camellias, rhododendrons and the like might be spectacular in their flowering season, but they take up a lot of space and most have little to offer for the rest of the year. Shrubs planted in borders – particularly in small gardens – really need to earn their space, so choose those that will go the extra mile and give more than just a short season of flower. The bonus might be long-lasting berries to follow the flowers, as with *Viburnum opulus* 'Compactum', or colourful foliage – for example, the golden leaves of *Philadelphus coronarius* 'Aureus', or the sophisticated black-purple ones of the cut-leaved ornamental elder *Sambucus nigra* 'Eva', which are such a great foil for both its own flowers and those of other plants.

Other flowering shrubs that really pay their way in a border are compact evergreens such as cistus, hebes, lavenders, santolinas and heathers. These work as ground cover and as foliage partners for other plants all through the year, as well as contributing colour in their own flowering season. Being relatively small, they are easy to work into planting schemes, either singly or in groups. Look out, too, for compact cultivars of lilac (*Syringa*),

A SUNNY BORDER IN AN OPEN SITE – 7 x 2.5m (23 x 8ft)

A double-aspect border in an open situation needs to look equally good from both sides. If taller plants are required for screening, place them along the middle of the bed. Use fairly hardy plants to withstand winter exposure as well as varieties that are tolerant of sun and wind. Similar planting on each side of the border can help it to link different areas of the garden, especially if you repeat a few of the plants and/or colours (here, blues and pinks, with purple and silver foliage) elsewhere.

1 *Cistus* × *lenis* 'Grayswood Pink' (x 2)
2 *Sambucus nigra* 'Eva' (x 2)
3 *Clematis* 'Petit Faucon' (x 2) (to scramble through no. 2)
4 *Convolvulus cneorum* (x 2)
5 *Tulipa praestans* (x 50)

6 *Weigela florida* 'Foliis Purpureis' (x 1)
7 *Euphorbia cyparissias* 'Fens Ruby' (x 3)
8 *Salvia* × *superba* (x 6)
9 *Caryopteris* × *clandonensis* 'Heavenly Blue' (x 4)
10 *Hebe* 'Great Orme' (x 2)

11 *Thymus serpyllum* 'Pink Chintz' (x 6)
12 *Hebe* 'Red Edge' (x 4)
13 *Stipa tenuissima* (x 9)
14 *Lavandula angustifolia* 'Royal Purple' (x 6)
15 *Daphne* × *burkwoodii* 'Somerset' (x 2)

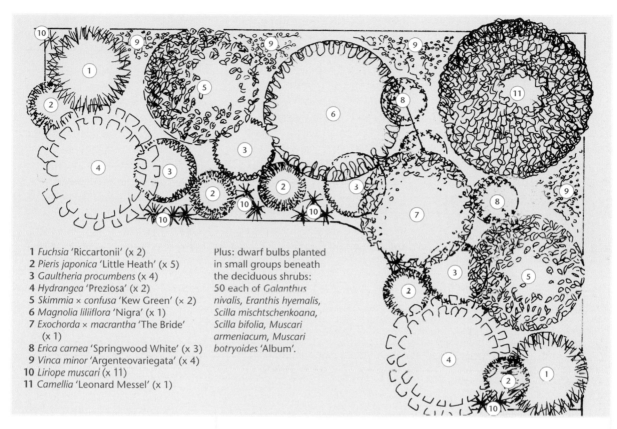

1 *Fuchsia* 'Riccartonii' (x 2)
2 *Pieris japonica* 'Little Heath' (x 5)
3 *Gaultheria procumbens* (x 4)
4 *Hydrangea* 'Preziosa' (x 2)
5 *Skimmia × confusa* 'Kew Green' (x 2)
6 *Magnolia liliiflora* 'Nigra' (x 1)
7 *Exochorda × macrantha* 'The Bride' (x 1)
8 *Erica carnea* 'Springwood White' (x 3)
9 *Vinca minor* 'Argenteovariegata' (x 4)
10 *Liriope muscari* (x 11)
11 *Camellia* 'Leonard Messel' (x 1)

Plus: dwarf bulbs planted in small groups beneath the deciduous shrubs: 50 each of *Galanthus nivalis, Eranthis hyemalis, Scilla mischtschenkoana, Scilla bifolia, Muscari armeniacum, Muscari botryoides* 'Album'.

A PARTIALLY SHADED CORNER BED ON ACID SOIL – 7 x 5M (23 x 16FT)
This west-facing border, sheltered from cold winds and the fiercest midday heat, features reds, deep pinks and purples to make the most of the late-afternoon sunshine. The planting includes a selection of the most sought-after acid-lovers: a camellia for early spring, a long-flowering magnolia, and two hydrangeas to make a good, rich, late-summer colour mix with fuchsias. Spring interest isn't forgotten, with dazzling white exochorda set against evergreen skimmias and pieris, and for the winter months there is ground cover consisting of white heather (*Erica*), variegated periwinkle (*Vinca*) and berrying gaultherias.

rhododendrons, philadelphus and other classic flowering shrubs. Their larger relatives may be fine for a spacious woodland setting where they don't need to worry about the neighbours, but useful little cultivars such as *Rhododendron* 'Ginny Gee' or *Syringa meyeri* 'Palibin' are better suited to the polite society of a garden border.

Sharing space
Although it's important not to overcrowd shrubs in a border, there are ways and means of fitting in more plants so that each shrub doesn't have to be the sole occupant of its space. Some climbers, such as summer-flowering clematis, are very happy to scramble through a spring-blossoming shrub, giving an additional season of interest. Two shrubs that flower at different seasons can overlap without a fight if you prune thoughtfully. This might, for example, entail cutting out some of the old flowered branches of a philadelphus immediately after it has flowered, to give more elbow room to a neighbouring buddleia that was hard pruned in early spring and is making rapid growth before its late-summer flowering.

Don't overlook the potential planting space underneath shrubs. Lots of early bulbs and perennials are never happier than when they're nestling underneath the branches of a deciduous shrub to give them shade in summer but plenty of sunshine and air in spring, when they're in flower (*see* pages 36–8).

Using bulbs in this way also neatly solves the problem of what to do with all that dying foliage after the bulbs have flowered: the shrubs will simply cover it up as they come into leaf and flower, and you can forget about it until next year. This is a useful trick with bold snowdrops like *Galanthus elwesii* or *Galanthus* 'Atkinsii' and dwarf daffodils such as *Narcissus* 'Tête-à-tête', 'Jack Snipe' and 'Jenny'. These are substantial

enough to make a real impact in a border, but it's easy for their fading foliage to spoil the fresh effect of later spring plants. And tidying up after them is a job you can do without, at a time of year when there's so much else to think about.

The back of the border

Some of the more vigorous flowering shrubs will soon cover an unsightly fence behind the border. Evergreens such as escallonia and camellia are especially useful in this respect and produce a spectacular backdrop. If space is tight, look to

early-flowering, upright shrubs to plant behind other things. Mahonias and *Daphne bholua* will both have flowered before many deciduous shrubs are waking up in spring – so can be seen in their full glory – but will be partially concealed later in the year by the plants in front of them. Remember that any plants you position on the shady side of a large shrub (especially an evergreen) will have to be pretty tolerant of low light conditions: a ceanothus planted behind a huge camellia or viburnum that cuts out the sun is unlikely to flower well.

A PARTIALLY SHADED WALL BORDER – 7 x 2.5M (23 x 8FT)

A border backed by a house wall lends itself to certain kinds of plants – trained wall shrubs, of course, like the flowering quince (*Chaenomeles*) here, but also fragrant plants such as a mock orange (*Philadelphus*) and daphne, whose scent can drift in through windows and doors. Make sure the plants and the wall complement each other: this scheme in mainly green, blue, creamy white and gold would suit brickwork, stone or render equally well.

Don't forget

Certain shrubs that would grow too large if left to their own devices can be used in borders if you keep them manageable by regular pruning of the right sort. Respect their natural shape and habit, and time your pruning to improve rather than curtail flowering (see pages 60–5).

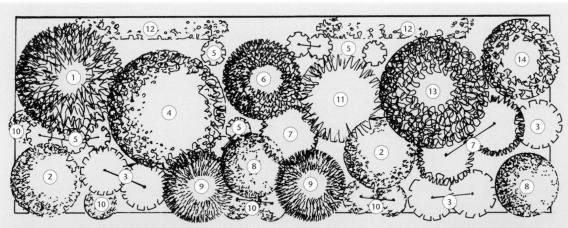

1 *Osmanthus heterophyllus* 'Variegatus' (x 1)
2 *Potentilla fruticosa* 'Tilford Cream' (x 2)
3 *Geranium* 'Jolly Bee' (x 5), underplanted with *Scilla siberica* (x 50)
4 *Philadelphus coronarius* 'Aureus' (x 1), underplanted with *Galanthus elwesii* (x 25)
5 *Aconitum* 'Spark's Variety' (x 9)

6 *Sarcococca confusa* (x 1)
7 *Campanula lactiflora* 'Prichard's Variety' (x 3)
8 *Buxus sempervirens* 'Elegantissima' (x 2)
9 *Hebe* 'Mrs Winder' (x 2)
10 *Veronica umbrosa* 'Georgia Blue' (× 6)

11 *Paeonia ludlowii* (x 1), underplanted with *Galanthus elwesii* (x 25)
12 *Chaenomeles speciosa* 'Nivalis' (trained on wall) (x 2), underplanted with *Narcissus* 'Jack Snipe' (x 50)
13 *Choisya* × *dewitteana* 'Aztec Pearl' (x 1)
14 *Daphne bholua* 'Darjeeling' (x 1)

Plants for a purpose

With so many options available, choosing flowering shrubs for specific purposes, conditions and effects can be quite a challenge. Use the lists in this section to help you find the right plant for the job. Refer, as well, to the A–Z directory of flowering shrubs on pages 77–107.

Like all the sun roses, *Cistus* × *hybridus* is drought-tolerant, so it will be happy in a warm, sunny spot in well-drained soil.

Best for hedges and screens

TALL SHRUBS

Berberis julianae
Escallonia 'Red Hedger'
Escallonia rubra 'Crimson Spire'
Forsythia × *intermedia* 'Lynwood Variety'
Olearia macrodonta
Viburnum tinus 'French White'

SHRUBS FOR LOW HEDGES

Fuchsia 'Riccartonii'
Hebe rakaiensis
Hydrangea macrophylla
Lavandula angustifolia 'Hidcote'
Potentilla fruticosa 'Vilmoriniana'
Rosmarinus officinalis
Viburnum tinus 'Eve Price'

Best for a focal point

Camellia japonica 'Adolphe Audusson'
Ceanothus 'Concha'
Cornus florida 'Cherokee Chief'
Cornus kousa var. *chinensis*
Hamamelis × *intermedia* 'Arnold Promise'
Hydrangea macrophylla 'Zorro'
Magnolia stellata 'Waterlily'
Mahonia × *media* 'Winter Sun'
Olearia × *scilloniensis* 'Dorrien-Smith'
Pieris floribunda 'Forest Flame'
Rhododendron 'Goldflimmer'
Viburnum plicatum f. *tomentosum* 'Mariesii'

Best dwarf shrubs for rock gardens and scree

Berberis thunbergii 'Admiration'
Calluna vulgaris 'Robert Chapman'
Daboecia cantabrica subsp. *scotica* 'Silverwells'
Erica carnea 'Vivellii'
Genista lydia
× *Halimiocistus* 'Ingwersenii'
Hebe 'Emerald Gem'
Helianthemum 'The Bride'
Phlomis fruticosa
Rhododendron 'Ginny Gee'
Rhododendron impeditum
Santolina chamaecyparissus 'Nana'
Spiraea japonica 'Golden Princess'
Thymus pulegioides 'Foxley'

Best for narrow borders

Caryopteris × *clandonensis* 'First Choice'
Chaenomeles speciosa 'Moerloosei'
Coronilla valentina subsp. *glauca*
Daphne mezereum
Forsythia × *intermedia* 'Week-End'
Fuchsia 'Tom Thumb'
Hebe 'Pewter Dome'
Hypericum olympicum f. *uniflorum* 'Citrinum'
Lavandula angustifolia 'Loddon Blue'
Rhododendron 'Patty Bee'
Syringa 'Red Pixie'

Best for cold, sunless sites

Cotoneaster horizontalis
Cotoneaster lacteus
Hydrangea arborescens 'Annabelle'
Hydrangea quercifolia
Hypericum androsaemum
Mahonia aquifolium
Mahonia japonica
Pyracantha 'Soleil d'Or'
Rhododendron 'Catawbiense Grandiflorum'
Rhododendron 'Cunningham's White'
Sarcococca confusa
Vinca minor 'Argenteovariegata'

Best for waterside sites

Amelanchier lamarckii
Clethra alnifolia
Cornus alba
Hydrangea macrophylla
Salix hastata
Sambucus racemosa
Sorbaria sorbifolia
Spiraea × *vanhouttei*
Viburnum opulus

Best for containers

Callistemon citrinus 'Splendens'
Camellia japonica 'Nuccio's Gem'
Cistus × *hybridus*
Convolvulus cneorum
Fuchsia 'Tom Thumb'
Hebe 'Silver Queen'
Hydrangea macrophylla 'Ami Pasquier'
Lavandula stoechas
Pieris japonica 'Little Heath'
Rhododendron 'Johanna'
Rhododendron 'Nancy Evans'
Skimmia japonica

Best for an upright habit

Camellia × williamsii 'Jury's Yellow'
Ceanothus 'Puget Blue'
Daphne bholua
Deutzia scabra 'Plena'
Hibiscus syriacus 'Hamabo'
Hydrangea paniculata 'Kyushu'
Kerria japonica 'Pleniflora'
Lavatera × clementii 'Rosea'
Magnolia 'Susan'
Philadelphus 'Virginal'
Ribes sanguineum 'Koja'
Rosmarinus officinalis 'Miss Jessopp's
   Upright'
Syringa × josiflexa 'Bellicent'

Best for an arching habit

Abelia × grandiflora 'Francis Mason'
Berberis × stenophylla
Buddleja alternifolia
Cornus kousa 'Miss Satomi'
Deutzia × hybrida 'Strawberry Fields'
Deutzia × rosea 'Carminea'
Exochorda × macrantha 'The Bride'
Fuchsia 'Mrs Popple'
Indigofera heterantha
Kolkwitzia amabilis
Osmanthus delavayi
Philadelphus 'Manteau d'Hermine'
Spiraea 'Arguta'

Best dome- and mound-forming shrubs

Ceanothus 'Blue Mound'
Cistus × obtusifolius 'Thrive'
Convolvulus cneorum
Cytisus × beanii
Genista lydia
Hebe 'Red Edge'
Lavandula angustifolia 'Imperial Gem'
Pieris japonica 'Debutante'
Potentilla fruticosa 'Elizabeth'
Rhododendron 'Dopey'
Rhododendron 'Scarlet Wonder'
Santolina chaemaecyparissus
Skimmia × confusa 'Kew Green'

Best low, carpeting shrubs

Calluna vulgaris 'Golden Carpet'
Ceanothus thyrsiflorus var. repens
Cornus canadensis
Cotoneaster dammeri
Erica carnea 'Springwood White'
Gaultheria procumbens
× Halimiocistus sahucii
Hebe pinguifolia 'Pagei'
Helianthemum 'Wisley Primrose'
Mahonia aquifolium 'Apollo'
Potentilla 'Medicine Wheel Mountain'
Rosmarinus officinalis Prostratus Group
Vinca minor 'La Grave'

Best for fruits and berries

Arctostaphylos uva-ursi
Berberis darwinii
Chaenomeles × superba 'Pink Lady'
Cornus mas
Cornus 'Porlock'
Cotoneaster frigidus 'Cornubia'
Daphne mezereum
Fatsia japonica
Gaultheria procumbens
Leycesteria formosa
Ribes odoratum
Skimmia japonica 'Veitchii'
Viburnum opulus 'Compactum'

Best for cutting to bring indoors

Abelia 'Edward Goucher'
Abeliophyllum distichum
Chimonanthus praecox
Choisya ternata
Erica × darleyensis
Forsythia × intermedia
Hydrangea macrophylla
Hypericum × inodorum
Lavandula × intermedia
Lonicera × purpusii
Sarcococca confusa
Skimmia japonica
Syringa vulgaris
Viburnum tinus

Best for fragrance

Abelia × grandiflora
Buddleja davidii 'Royal Red'
Chimonanthus praecox
Choisya × dewitteana 'Aztec Pearl'
Cytisus battandieri
Daphne bholua 'Jacqueline Postill'
Lonicera × purpusii 'Winter Beauty'
Mahonia japonica
Myrtus communis
Osmanthus delavayi
Philadelphus 'Belle Etoile'
Sarcococca confusa
Skimmia × confusa 'Kew Green'
Spartium junceum
Syringa vulgaris 'Madame Lemoine'
Viburnum × burkwoodii
Viburnum carlesii 'Diana'

Best for colourful foliage

YELLOW
Choisya ternata 'Sundance'
Philadelphus coronarius 'Aureus'
Sambucus racemosa 'Sutherland Gold'
Spiraea japonica 'Firelight'
Weigela 'Briant Rubidor'

RED OR PURPLE
Cornus florida 'Sunset'
Hebe 'Mrs Winder'
Sambucus nigra 'Eva'

VARIEGATED OR MIXED COLOURS
Cornus mas 'Variegata'
Pieris japonica 'Carnival'
Weigela 'Koseriana Variegata'

AUTUMN COLOUR
Ceratostigma willmottianum
Clethra alnifolia 'Paniculata'
Cotoneaster horizontalis
Enkianthus campanulatus
Fothergilla major
Hamamelis × intermedia 'Jelena'
Hydrangea 'Preziosa'
Itea virginica 'Henry's Garnet'
Rhododendron luteum
Viburnum opulus

Hydrangea macrophylla 'Mariesii Perfecta' will tolerate pollution and is an ideal shrub for a container in a city garden.

Best for evergreen foliage

Berberis darwinii
Brachyglottis (Dunedin Group) 'Sunshine'
Camellia japonica 'Elegans'
Choisya ternata
Escallonia 'Iveyi'
Hebe 'Midsummer Beauty'
Magnolia grandiflora 'Exmouth'
Mahonia lomariifolia
Myrtus communis
Pieris japonica 'Katsura'
Pittosporum tobira
Rhododendron 'Goldflimmer'
Rhododendron 'Horizon Monarch'

Fastest-growing

Buddleja davidii 'White Profusion'
Ceanothus thyrsiflorus 'Skylark'
Cotoneaster frigidus 'Cornubia'
Deutzia × *hybrida* 'Magicien'
Fuchsia 'Riccartonii'
Lavatera × *clementii* 'Barnsley'
Sambucus nigra f. *laciniata*
Viburnum × *bodnantense* 'Dawn'
Viburnum opulus 'Roseum'

Most long-flowering

Ceanothus × *delileanus* 'Gloire de Versailles'
Escallonia 'Pride of Donard'
Fuchsia 'Riccartonii'
× *Halimiocistus* 'Ingwersenii'
Hebe 'Great Orme'
Hydrangea serrata 'Bluebird'
Hypericum 'Hidcote'
Leycesteria formosa
Potentilla fruticosa 'Primrose Beauty'
Viburnum tinus 'Eve Price'

Most drought-tolerant

Berberis × *stenophylla*
Buddleja alternifolia
Ceanothus 'Autumnal Blue'
Cistus × *purpureus*
Convolvulus cneorum
Cotoneaster horizontalis
Fuchsia magellanica
Lavandula angustifolia 'Munstead'
Philadelphus 'Beauclerk'
Phlomis fruticosa
Potentilla 'Goldfinger'
Rosmarinus officinalis

Most vandal-proof

Berberis darwinii
Berberis × *stenophylla*
Chaenomeles × *superba*
Mahonia japonica
Mahonia × *media* 'Charity'
Osmanthus heterophyllus 'Gulftide'
Ulex europaeus

Most pollution-tolerant

Amelanchier lamarckii
Buddleja davidii 'Black Knight'
Cistus × *dansereaui* 'Decumbens'
Cytisus × *praecox* 'Allgold'
Deutzia × *hybrida* 'Mont Rose'
Forsythia × *intermedia* 'Spectabilis'
Hebe pinguifolia 'Pagei'
Hibiscus syriacus 'Oiseau Bleu'
Hydrangea macrophylla 'Mariesii Perfecta'
Kerria japonica 'Golden Guinea'
Philadelphus 'Minnesota Snowflake'
Ribes sanguineum 'King Edward VII'
Spiraea × *vanhoutteii*
Syringa vulgaris 'Charles Joly'
Weigela 'Bristol Ruby'

Planting and growing

Most flowering shrubs are hardy creatures that thrive in gardens regardless of neglect and even a little rough treatment. However, to get the best from them you need to give them a good start in life and be prepared to bestow a little TLC upon them – just occasionally – over the years. If you do, they will reward with a lavish display of flowers with amazing reliability.

Tools and equipment

If growing flowering shrubs, you'll need to invest in a set of good-quality tools. A spade is vital for planting new shrubs in the open ground, and a hand fork is a must for general cultivation, under and between established shrubs. However, the most essential equipment you need to keep flowering shrubs in peak condition is a pruning kit: secateurs are essential, loppers desirable, and a pruning saw an advantage when dealing with overgrown specimens.

Pruning buddleia with secateurs. Last year's stems are easily cut back using a sharp-bladed pair of bypass secateurs.

Secateurs

Secateurs are used for cutting woody shoots up to about 1cm (½in) thick. Buy a good-quality pair that you find comfortable and easy to use. To the serious gardener, a fine pair of bypass pruners, those where the blades cross each other as they cut in a scissor action, are lifetime companions and well worth the investment. Anvil secateurs work slightly differently: they have one sharp blade that closes down onto a flat edge, rather like a guillotine. Bypass secateurs are preferable to anvil types, particularly for cutting hollow or brittle-stemmed plants, as they make a neater cut.

Gardeners who find pruning difficult, perhaps because of arthritic hands, might like to consider secateurs with rolling handles. They cause much less repetitive strain to your hand when you're doing a lot of pruning work. Ratchet secateurs,

where the blades are drawn together in stages, are another type that is worth considering.

To protect hands and lower arms when using secateurs, a sturdy pair of gardening gloves is essential.

Loppers

Loppers are basically secateurs with long handles and are useful for cutting stems or branches about 1–2.5cm (½–1in) thick. In addition, they reduce the amount of bending and reaching you need to do. The long handles allow you to reach into the middle of a shrub to cut out branches without battling your way in with a pair of secateurs. Consider a thorny subject like berberis and you can see the advantage! As with secateurs, both bypass and anvil loppers are available. Anvil loppers can be easier to use when cutting through woody stems because of their greater leverage.

Long-handled loppers are useful when cutting flowered stems low down or in the centre of the shrub.

Don't forget

A sharp pruning saw is useful when cutting back large woody shrubs. Choose one with a curved blade – it's easier to make a clean cut without slipping down the branch as you saw.

Growing conditions

Few gardeners have perfect soil – that deep, well-drained, fertile soil that we all read about in gardening books. However, the majority of flowering shrubs aren't that fussy; they tend to grow on most soils, providing they're reasonably fertile and well drained. The exceptions are the ericaceous plants: rhododendrons, azaleas, camellias and pieris. They will grow only in acid soil. If you're not sure of your soil type, you need to check it.

Testing your soil

If the plants in your garden grow well and look healthy, there's no need to do a comprehensive soil test. You can supply any nutrients that could be lacking by general feeding (*see* page 56). If plants struggle to get going, and look pale

A simple soil-test kit. Mix a sample of soil with water, and the chemical in the test tube, and it changes colour. Compare it with the colour chart supplied to see what the pH is.

Know your soil

If you're unsure of your soil type, the simplest test of all is to go out into the garden on a dry day, pick up a handful, give it a squeeze, then open your hand. Take a close look at the colour and texture of the soil.

① Loam is mid- to dark brown and feels soft and crumbly. Depending on how dry it is, it might form a soft clump.

② Clay soil may be greyish rather than brown. It will form a clod in your hand and feels sticky.

③ Peaty soil is dark, soft and spongy. If it's wet you might get some drops of water out of it as you squeeze.

④ Sandy soil will slip through your fingers and feels rough and gritty.

⑤ Chalky soil is pale or greyish brown, which should give you a clue before you squeeze. It's slightly gritty with white fragments in it and is crumbly so will not form a clump.

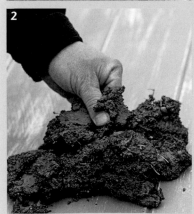

and fragile, it might be worth doing a soil test, which will tell you the nutrient content of the soil and its pH – the measure of acidity or alkalinity. Simple soil-testing kits are available from any garden centre.

Ericaceous plants, such as rhododendrons and camellias, will not grow on soil with a high pH – that is, alkaline soils. In these conditions, essential nutrients become unavailable to them. If you're unsure, do a soil test or buy a pH meter. The latter is a spike that you push into the soil with a simple gauge that tells you the pH. If the reading is below 7, it's acid; if above, it's alkaline – simple as that.

Digging

Digging and turning over the soil before planting will reap rewards later. Some soils may look good on the surface but deeper down they may be compacted: hard and impenetrable to plant roots. By opening up the structure with a fork, you allow air to penetrate and water to drain freely. Digging clay soils can be hard and heavy work but it's easier if you use one of the narrower, lighter styles of spade rather than one of the broader, heavier types, as you'll be lifting lighter loads.

It's also a good idea to fork lightly around established shrubs occasionally – this breaks up the soil surface, enabling water and air to

The addition of plenty of well-rotted garden compost or manure at the time of planting or as a mulch around existing shrubs is the secret of success. Break it up well in a wheelbarrow before you use it – lovely stuff!

get to the roots more easily. It's best to do this after you've applied fertilizer or a mulch of garden compost or manure.

Improving the soil

Nearly all soils are improved by the addition of organic matter in the form of good garden compost or well-rotted manure. Organic matter boosts the humus content of the soil; humus is the slightly sticky, liquid part of the soil that clings around the mineral soil particles keeping them apart, but hanging on to water and nutrients at the same time. By adding organic matter, you turn heavy clay or dry, chalky soil into deep, well-drained, fertile soil that your flowering shrubs will love.

Before planting, add lots of compost or manure and dig it in well. Your established shrubs will also appreciate liberal amounts of compost or manure added to the soil surface; this will gradually work its way down to the roots. The addition of organic matter to the soil is not a once-in-a-lifetime thing. The more often you do it, the better the growing conditions will be.

The only soils that don't benefit from lots of organic matter are dark, peaty soils (*see* opposite), which are already high in organic matter and low in nutrients. They usually benefit from the addition of fertilizers (*see* page 56); also, it's important to choose flowering shrubs that succeed on them – often ericaceous subjects.

> ### Don't forget
> If you're not sure of your soil type or what will grow in your garden, take a good look around neighbouring gardens and see what thrives there. What grows well in their soil conditions will normally thrive in yours.

Choosing flowering shrubs

There's a fantastic variety of flowering shrubs available to the gardener. Garden centres and nurseries are positively bursting with exciting possibilities and, as they're cultivated in containers, you can buy them at different stages of maturity at any time of the year. New varieties are introduced all the time – so keep an open mind and you might find something even better than the plant you were originally looking for.

Size of plant

Flowering shrubs are often offered in more than one size. Larger plants cost more, but you don't have to wait as long for them to make an impact in your garden. Smaller plants offer good value and mean you have some change to spend on other plants. Find out which shrubs grow quickly and which take time, and if you do go for larger specimens choose those plants that take longer to reach maturity. It's also worth buying larger plants where instant impact is needed:

A great selection of flowering shrubs is available from garden centres and nurseries throughout the year. Buy one because you like it, but also consider how it will fit into your garden scheme and whether you can provide the conditions it needs.

Shrubs to buy in flower

Camellia japonica

Cistus

Fuchsia

Hamamelis × intermedia

Hibiscus syriacus

Hydrangea macrophylla

Magnolia stellata

Mahonia

Potentilla arbuscula

Rhododendron

maybe to fill a hole in the border where another plant has failed.

It's not worth buying larger specimens of short-lived plants such as lavenders and lavateras. Smaller specimens give better results.

What to look for

■ Before buying, check the plant is suitable for the position in the garden you have in mind. Plant labels give useful basic information, but they're only a guide.

■ Look for healthy, well-cared-for shrubs that haven't been hanging around in their pots for a long time. It's easy to tell if they have: they often have yellowing leaves, poor top-growth and just look too big for their containers.

■ Choose a specimen with a good shape and strong branches – once the flowers have died off, you'll be left with the shrub's framework the rest of the year.

■ Select plants with a healthy, developed root system and avoid pot-bound specimens. Invert the pot and check the roots; a congested mass indicates a plant is pot bound.

■ The surface of the compost should be free of weeds and algae.

■ Where a large number of different varieties of a plant are available it may be best to buy when in flower (*see* box, left). That way, you can be certain you're getting the colour, form or fragrance you want.

Planting flowering shrubs

Traditionally, flowering shrubs were planted during autumn, winter and early spring, when deciduous subjects were dormant and evergreens were producing little growth. Now that shrubs are grown and sold in pots, they can be planted at any time of the year, but remember that planting when the shrubs are growing, and possibly flowering, in late spring and summer means they need extra aftercare, particularly watering.

Planting in open ground

The future success of a shrub depends upon its successful establishment; in other words, the development of the root system to support the stems, leaves and flowers above ground. As a gardener, you need to encourage this by giving the plant the best possible start for root development.

First, you need to decide if where you're planning to plant the shrub has enough space for it to mature. If not, you'll need to choose a different plant or make the space larger. It's always difficult to imagine that little plant in a pot, or that bare stick with a few roots, will ever make a shrub over a metre in height and spread – but it will!

Next, water the shrub thoroughly, wetting the rootball right through. If you don't, the roots will probably stay dry even after planting.

When conditions are good, prepare the ground and add plenty of organic matter (*see* page 49). Then prepare the planting hole: this must be much bigger than the rootball is now. Dig the hole at least four times the width of the rootball and at least twice the depth (*see* page 52). This allows you to add compost and fertilizer to the soil that you will replace in the planting hole.

You then plant your shrub to the same depth as it was growing in the container. Don't bury it or leave it perched above the surface. Firm the soil around the roots using your fist, toe or heel but take care not to damage the plant.

Water the shrub again thoroughly. You need to water whatever time of year you're planting, even during the winter months, so that the roots don't dry out and can become established. Give the plant a really good soaking.

You should avoid planting in frosty conditions, as much for your comfort as for the well-being of your plants, since frosty ground can be very hard to dig. However, frost rarely persists for long periods and once your shrubs are in the ground, frost is unlikely to harm them.

It's also advisable to avoid planting during drought conditions. Wait until rain has moistened the soil thoroughly and has had time to drain away from the surface.

Filling gaps between newly planted shrubs

Make sure you leave enough distance between newly planted shrubs to give them room to grow. Even small shrubs, such as cistus, hebes and spiraeas, will ultimately have a spread of a metre or so; therefore, you need to plant 1m (40in) apart. This will leave gaps in the first few seasons, which can be filled with annuals for summer colour. Plants such as snapdragons (*Antirrhinum*), salvias and tobacco

Container-grown shrubs are easy to plant, but good preparation and planting is key to their future success. Do not forget to leave them enough room to grow and mature.

HOW TO plant a shrub in the ground

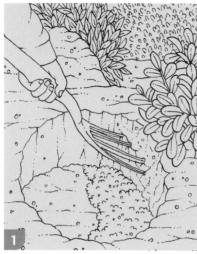

Dig a big planting hole at least four times the width of the rootball and at least twice the depth. Use a fork to free up the soil at the sides and base of the hole, and mix compost and a general fertilizer with the soil you have removed.

If the roots are tightly packed around the sides of the rootball, loosen the outer ones to help them to move out into the ground. Be careful not to damage the fleshy roots of shrubs such as magnolias, which could delay flowering.

Replace some prepared soil in the hole and position the shrub in the centre, making sure it is at the same depth in the soil as it was in its pot. Placing a cane across the planting hole makes it easier to judge this.

Replace the prepared soil around the roots of the shrub and firm with your fist or foot. Leave a saucer-shaped depression around the shrub to make watering easier. Water thoroughly after planting and in the next few months until the shrub is established.

plants (*Nicotiana*) mix happily with flowering shrubs; they're taller and less formal than compact bedding subjects. Hardy annuals like *Nigella*, *Clarkia* and *Godetia* can be sown direct into open ground in spaces between shrubs. They grow and flower in a few weeks and will often seed themselves to reappear the following year.

It's also a good idea to underplant deciduous flowering shrubs with evergreen ground-cover plants. These help to fill the gaps while newly planted shrubs are maturing, and hopefully they will suppress weed growth. They also add interest to the border once the leaves of the shrubs fall in winter. Good plants to choose include bugle (*Ajuga*), sedge (*Carex*), *Heuchera*, *Pachysandra* and periwinkle (*Vinca*).

Planting shrubs in pots

Many shrubs, particularly evergreens, make excellent permanent subjects for containers. When choosing a pot, buy one that is big enough to allow the plant to develop. If you're going to grow it on and move it into a larger container in future (*see* opposite), consider the shape of this first pot. Those that are narrow at the top make it virtually impossible to remove the plant without damaging it and the pot. Also,

Planting bare-root shrubs

Some shrubs, particularly some hedging plants and roses, are usually planted as 'bare-roots' during the autumn and winter months. If the roots are dry, soak them in a bucket of water for a few hours before planting. Spread the roots out as much as possible in the planting hole and plant firmly.

remember that small pots dry out quickly and blow over, and some containers are damaged by frost.

For most flowering shrubs, you can use a multipurpose compost when planting up containers, but you'll get better results with loam-based compost, such as John Innes. This has finer particles that hang on to water and nutrients more successfully. Use John Innes No. 3 for most flowering shrubs, but not for ericaceous plants. To grow a camellia, rhododendron, azalea or pieris in a pot, use a peat-free ericaceous compost.

The principles of planting in a container are just the same as those for planting in open ground: you need to water the plant before and after planting; plant to the same depth that the plant was growing in its original pot, and firm the compost gently around the rootball.

In future years

Flowering shrubs benefit from repotting every three years or so. However, there comes a point where you can't keep on repotting a plant: the job becomes unmanageable, and you simply can't find a pot large enough. You can keep the shrub healthy and encourage flowering by top-dressing each spring. Scrape away the upper layer of compost (about 5cm/2in) and replace it with fresh compost and fertilizer.

Don't forget

Shrubs in containers will need feeding because the nutrients in the compost are quickly used up or washed away by watering. A controlled- or slow-release granular fertilizer is ideal, as you only have to add it once or twice a year.

HOW TO repot a container-grown shrub

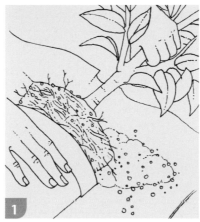

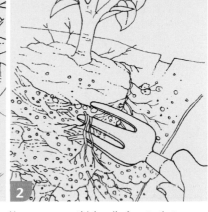

1 Lay the shrub on its side and gently slip the pot away from the plant. If the plant is wedged in firmly, you'll need to loosen the rootball first by tapping the container rim with a block of wood or sliding a long knife between the pot and the compost. Alternatively, use a hose on a low-pressure setting to wash the roots away from the sides of the container.

2 You may see a thick coil of roots that form a solid pot shape around the plant, depending on how pot bound it is. Using a hand fork, gently prise the congested roots from the solid mass so that they can grow into the surrounding compost once replanted in the new container. Any thick roots that will make repotting difficult can be shortened.

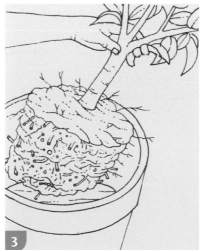

3 Prepare the new, slightly larger pot for planting. Place a layer of mesh then a layer of crocks at the base of the pot, covering the drainage hole, then add a layer of potting compost to cover. Place the plant in the centre of the pot, spreading out the roots.

4 Fill the gap between the pot and the plant with more compost, firming lightly. When potting is complete, the surface of the rootball should be about 2.5–5cm (1–2in) below the rim of the pot to allow for watering. You can prune the top-growth by about one third (*see* page 64).

Moving established shrubs

Sometimes an established shrub is just in the wrong place. Maybe it has outgrown its position, or perhaps the layout of the garden has changed. You might want to relocate the plant to a new position or even a different garden. In most cases, it's possible to move a shrub if you go about it in the right way, and providing it's not too awkward to handle.

Secrets of success

The time to move an established shrub is when growth has slowed down, or the plant is dormant, from late autumn to early spring. The roots will be damaged during the moving process, so the earlier in the season you do it the better; the roots then have time to re-establish themselves in the new location before growth resumes in spring.

When moving larger established shrubs, you make the job easier and increase the chances of success if you reduce the top-growth by pruning. As a rule of thumb, reducing the branches by one third will compensate for the root loss the plant will suffer when lifted.

Obviously, the more of the rootball you can keep intact the better. A systematic approach, as shown in these illustrations, is key.

Is it worth moving?

Not all mature flowering shrubs are worth moving. Some are short-lived and have a root system that never makes a solid rootball. Brooms

HOW TO move an established shrub

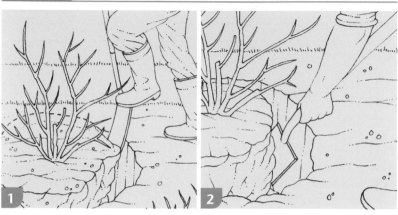

1 Using a sharp spade, dig a trench around the shrub. This should be to the depth of the spade blade and in line with the extent of the branches – or further away from the centre if the shrub is small.

Use the spade to cut horizontally, or at an angle of 45 degrees, under the rootball of the shrub until the shrub is separated from the ground and sitting on an 'island' of soil in the centre of the hole.

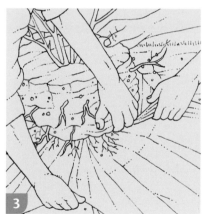

3 Slide a thick sheet of polythene or a large piece of sacking under the rootball. Do this by carefully lifting one side of the shrub's rootball and gradually working the sheet underneath. This is easier with two people.

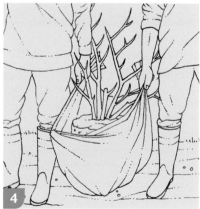

4 Gather the corners of the sheet and use it to lift the plant out of its hole and transport it to the new planting position. Careful soil preparation, planting and watering after replanting will ensure the operation is a success (*see* page 52).

(*Cytisus*), for example, are never worth moving. Nor are lavateras, cistus, lavenders and ceanothus, because they're relatively short-lived and you'd get better results by planting a new small specimen.

Ericaceous subjects like camellias and rhododendrons, on the other hand, have compact, fibrous root systems and tend to move happily even as large mature specimens a few years down the line.

Watering

Most established flowering shrubs don't need regular watering, except perhaps in drought conditions. However, you do need to pay particular attention to watering while a new or relocated plant becomes established; this is vital to its future success. You also need to water containers and raised beds regularly. Supply water, too, to shrubs facing competition from neighbouring trees and hedges; these suck up the available water in the soil before your flowering shrubs can get at it.

Watering methods

Watering anything in the garden is a chore if the water is hard to get at. If you have to squeeze your watering can under the kitchen tap, or you have to feed your hosepipe through the bathroom window, you'll avoid using it. Therefore, an outside tap is really an essential in any garden. This must run off the mains supply, and not be water that has passed through a softener.

If you have quite a few plants in your garden and know you'll need to water regularly, buy a good-quality hosepipe and reel. A hosepipe that kinks and knots is worse than no hosepipe at all. Alternatively, buy yourself a nice, big, well-balanced watering can.

The secret of successful watering is how you deliver it to the roots of the plant. You need gentle, gradual delivery that soaks into the ground where you direct it – at the roots. A flash flood of water fired onto the ground runs away over the soil surface and does not do the job. If

you're watering by hand, buy a good-quality hose-end attachment.

Alternatively, consider a seep (or soaker) hose. This is a perforated rubber tube that you lay on the soil surface. The water gently seeps from the hose into the ground. This is ideal if you're planting a number of shrubs close together or establishing a new bed. It's also a great way to maintain a newly planted hedge.

Conserving water

No one wants to waste water, and you don't have to be extravagant with it in the garden. Every garden should have a water butt to capture rainwater from a downpipe from the

An old barrel makes an excellent water butt. Remember to raise it off the ground so that you can fit your watering can under the tap.

roof of the house or an outbuilding. You can use some water from the house on established shrubs in your garden. Water used for washing vegetables is ideal. Avoid any water that contains excessive detergents, but you could certainly use your bathwater as long as you don't use bubblebath or too much soap.

Mulching the ground around your flowering shrubs with compost or bark earlier in the season will also help to conserve moisture and reduce watering (*see* pages 57–8).

Don't forget

Generally, flowering shrubs are robust, woody plants that do not require regular watering. Don't water unless necessary – all you'll achieve is more soft, leafy growth, meaning the plant needs even more water to support it. Also, if you encourage soft, vigorous growth that usually means fewer flowers.

An upturned plastic water bottle, with the base cut out, makes an excellent funnel to direct water straight to the roots of a newly planted shrub.

Feeding

Although your soil probably contains enough nutrients to support plant growth, to get the best out of your flowering shrubs you'll need to mulch them with compost or manure and feed them with fertilizer – once or twice a year for best results. Most gardeners choose a general fertilizer that contains all of the main plant nutrients plus trace elements: the vitamins and minerals in a plant's diet that keep it in tip-top condition.

Plant nutrition

The main plant nutrients are nitrogen, phosphorus (phosphate) and potassium (potash). Nitrogen (N) is used for leaf and stem growth, phosphorus (P) for root development, and potassium (K) for flower and fruit production. The proportion of each in a fertilizer determines the sort of growth it will promote. Look on the packet to find out the ratio and select one that is most suited to your requirements. When planting flowering shrubs, phosphorus is the important ingredient to ensure good root development. To promote prolific flowering, potassium is essential. General slow-release fertilizers, such as fish, blood and bone, contain equal amounts of each, so are ideal for general feeding. For acid-loving plants such as rhododendrons and camellias, you must choose a peat- free ericaceous fertilizer.

Types of fertilizer

Fertilizers come in a variety of formulations and types that can be applied in different ways. There are organic fertilizers (made from plant or animal derivatives) and inorganic (chemical) fertilizers. Both need to be used in damp soil.

A powdered or granular fertilizer is the ideal choice for feeding your shrubs in early spring, and perhaps again in summer, especially if they flower for a second time in autumn. You simply sprinkle a handful or two over the soil surface around each plant. Try to distribute it around the drip line of the shrub – that is, the point where the branches extend to. This is where the roots are

Liquid fertilizers are useful to give plants a boost or to quickly supply a nutrient that is lacking.

Don't forget

Many fertilizers can affect the soil's pH level (see pages 48–9). For example, many chemical types make the soil more acidic.

most active and the fertilizer will be most effective.

Liquid fertilizers, which you dilute in a watering can and use when the plant is in growth, make nutrients available to the plant immediately in the soil water. They are generally used for shrubs only when a plant needs a tonic or is lacking a particular nutrient.

Controlled-release fertilizers, with clever little granules that release nutrients only when the weather is warm enough and the soil is moist enough, are ideal to feed flowering shrubs growing in containers. You need to apply them only once a year, in spring.

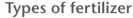

A slow-release fertilizer is sprinkled onto the soil surface and then worked into the ground using a fork or hoe.

Weed control and mulching

Flowering shrubs are the backbone of the border – they keep the whole planting scheme on track throughout the year, so it's vital to keep them in tip-top shape, without any competition from weeds. Mulching around shrubs will help to suppress weed growth and is beneficial in several other ways, too. A mulch applied early on will mean less work later.

Weed control

Once shrubs become established and provide effective ground cover, you will have few problems from weeds. It is bare soil between plants that presents the opportunity for weeds to develop. So if you get your plant spacing right, and the shrubs join up as they mature, there is no room for weeds to grow. However, until that ideal situation is reached, the bare soil between shrubs offers the perfect opportunity for annual and perennial weeds to take hold.

The problem is always greater where there was a weed infestation before the shrubs were planted. The secret of success is to get rid of the weeds as part of the pre-planting process. All gardeners are keen to get planting, whether it is a single shrub in the border or a whole new bed or garden area. However, if you have a weed problem it's vital to sort it out before you plant.

Applying a mulch onto clean, moist ground between shrubs and perennials helps to conserve moisture and suppresses weed growth.

Annual weeds

Annual weeds, like groundsel, are a short-term problem. Their seeds are brought to the surface when the soil is disturbed by digging. To get rid of them you need to kill them or dig them up before they set seed, and because they grow, flower and set seed quickly, it's important not to hang around. A hoe is your secret weapon: use it to chop them off when young and they wither and die quickly. While the ground is weed-free, cover the surface with a mulch of chipped bark. This will bury other annual weed seeds and prevent them from germinating.

Perennial weeds

Perennial weeds are a different matter. They grow and multiply, and their roots persist in the soil. They're difficult to eradicate when they become established between mature plants. Even if you manage to remove the leaves and stems, they grow again from the roots, which are often entwined around the roots of your shrubs and perennials.

To control them you either have to dig them out completely, if possible, or use a systemic weedkiller that you apply to the leaves and shoots of the weed and it passes

Established clumps of bramble, a perennial weed, spread via arching, thorny stems that root at their tips, forming an impenetrable thicket.

Cleavers is an annual, sticky-stemmed weed that quickly scrambles through flowering shrub borders in areas of shade. It sets seed freely.

Bindweed is a pernicious perennial climber that spreads by creeping roots that may run more than 60cm (2ft) deep. It is very difficult to remove.

down the plant to kill the roots. This may take quite a lot of patience and skill as you might have to unravel climbing weeds such as bindweed from the branches of shrubs, or shield plants with a piece of cardboard or plastic while you carefully spray the weeds.

Needless to say, it's much easier to control perennial weeds before you plant, so if they're present, get rid of them when preparing the soil.

Mulching

Applying mulch around shrubs is hugely beneficial because it's a way of adding organic matter to the soil, and it conserves moisture, thereby reducing the need for watering. It also suppresses weed growth. What's more, if you do it well, a mulch looks good and sets your shrubs off a treat. The secret of success is to make sure you spread mulch on weed-free ground and

when the soil is moist, early or late in the year; by midsummer, the lighter rains might not be able to penetrate it.

Types of mulch

Today, when we think of mulch we usually think of chipped bark. There are a great many different grades available; those with larger, heavier chips are longer-lasting and do not blow around as easily. Bark is really successful only on level sites. If you use it on a slope, it quickly slips down to the bottom.

Leaf mould makes a wonderful mulch that your flowering shrubs will really enjoy. Gather up fallen leaves in autumn and put them into plastic sacks and stack them in a shady corner out of sight. In a year or so, the leaves will have broken down to a lovely, rich organic mulch. Leaf mould also makes an excellent soil improver.

If you use your own garden compost as mulch, make sure it's weed-free. Try it on a small area to start with and leave it for two or three weeks before you spread it around. You don't want to introduce more weeds.

Garden centres sell all manner of different mulching materials in nice, easy-to-handle bags. You'll find mulches made of recycled green waste, straw, chipped wood and paper waste, to name but a few.

You can also use grass cuttings as mulch under large, established shrubs and hedges, providing that you do not heap the cuttings up around the base of the stems and you do not use too thick a layer.

Don't forget

For a layer of mulch to be successful, it needs to be thick enough to cover the surface. An 8cm (3in) depth over the soil is the minimum. A thin layer, where the soil shows through in areas, is a waste of money and effort.

Most flowering shrubs are perfectly hardy and, in British gardens, they will come through the winter unscathed. Some, however, especially certain delicate evergreens, can be damaged by freezing weather, especially in exposed, windy situations.

Slightly tender evergreens, such as large-leaved hebes, are easily damaged by frost during the winter months.

Frost damage

Frost damage shows up in a variety of ways. Evergreen leaves may appear scorched and blackened, especially around the edges, after exposure to frost. This may be made worse if they thaw out quickly in the morning sun. Once leaves are damaged in this way you just have to wait for a flush of new growth in spring to put things right.

In severe cases it is the stems that are damaged. Water in the vessels that transport it up the plant simply freezes, causing them to burst, just like the pipes in your house. This results in irreparable damage and you have to cut out the frost-damaged growth.

Preventing frost damage

Evergreen shrubs with soft, lush growth, and deciduous shrubs with soft, unripened shoots are easily damaged by frost. Avoid high-nitrogen fertilizers, like farmyard manure, in autumn as this can stimulate growth when the plant should be dormant. High-potash fertilizers will harden growth and make them more resistant. Pruning evergreens late in the growing season can also stimulate growth, resulting in soft young shoots that are prone to damage.

The simplest way to protect a shrub from frost is using horticultural fleece. This light, permeable fabric holds an insulating layer of air around the plant when it is lightly draped over the shrub and secured by tying it to the branches just above soil level. There are heavier and lighter grades of fleece. The heavy

Snow does not usually cause cold-damage to evergreens – in fact, it creates a layer of insulation. However, when the thaw comes the weight of it can break branches.

ones give greater protection, but can stimulate premature growth if the weather warms up. The great benefit of using fleece is that it reduces wind chill and therefore limits potential damage to the plant. Fleece is easy to attach around wall shrubs, but can be tricky to keep in place around freestanding subjects. Look out for tubes of fleece that you just slip over your precious shrubs.

Smaller, newly planted evergreens can be protected by lightly heaping straw around the plants and keeping it in position with a tube of wire mesh.

Plants in containers are particularly susceptible to root damage. As the soil freezes, tender root-tips around the edges of the pot are frozen and killed. You can prevent this by lagging the pot with horticultural fleece, sacking, or straw in plastic sacks. Bubble wrap, used for packaging and insulating greenhouses, is very effective when wrapped around the pot, over the compost and secured around the base of the shrub (*see* left). The compost can be covered for a few days at a time.

There are various ways to protect shrubs.
① Bubble wrap is effective when used to insulate pots containing shrubs.
② Straw can be heaped around smaller evergreen shrubs.

Pruning

By pruning flowering shrubs, you can greatly improve their performance in the garden; it can also ruin them if you get it wrong. Perhaps this is why gardeners are often nervous about pruning. However, there is no need to be. If you approach the task logically, and remember a few simple rules, it is easy. Never prune just for the sake of it, always do it for a reason.

Viburnums do not need regular pruning. However, this mature specimen has grown so well over the years that a tall stepladder and loppers are needed to trim back the upper branches to control its spread and keep the plant flowering.

There are a number of reasons why you prune flowering shrubs. The most important is to encourage flowering. If you prune at the right time of the year, you will encourage new growth that will flower well the following season. Therefore, always prune soon after flowering. If you prune several months after flowering you will be cutting off the growth that may already have formed flower buds.

You might also prune to control size and shape. This is where many gardeners get carried away and spoil the effect because they are too controlling. In some cases, regular pruning is necessary if you want to achieve a formal look. But this does not suit many flowering shrubs which look better, and flower better, if you preserve their natural shape.

Whether you prune for these reasons or not, you will still need to remove dead, damaged and diseased wood on occasions, to keep your shrubs healthy and looking good.

Formative pruning

Formative pruning influences the shape and habit of a plant. You prune to encourage the plant to grow in a particular way. The most important thing to remember is that hard pruning encourages strong, vigorous growth. Light pruning, on the other hand, encourages twiggy, less vigorous growth.

Think about what you want the plant to do. Young, newly planted shrubs often benefit from hard pruning early in life to encourage growth and branching low down. Formative pruning of mature shrubs might involve selective removal of some of the stems to create a stronger, more attractive branch framework.

Remember, wherever you cut, those buds behind the cut will grow and develop to produce new stems. Look at the direction they're likely to grow in, and you'll have a good idea of the subsequent shape of that part of the plant.

Maintenance pruning

Maintenance pruning involves the removal of old flowerheads and stems, and dead and diseased wood. This is usually light work on low-growing and young shrubs, but might involve more major annual pruning of mature specimens.

You should remove faded flowers and old flowered stems after flowering, and this is the major pruning time for most flowering shrubs. However, it's still a good idea to revisit deciduous flowering shrubs in winter, free of leaves, when it's much easier to see any damaged stems that need removing.

Some plants don't need regular pruning at all (*see* box, below).

How to prune

Most pruning is done using a pair of secateurs (or pruners). For best results, use a good-quality tool with

Where to cut the stem

Where the plant has opposite buds, make a horizontal cut straight across the stem, just above a pair of buds. Where a plant has alternate buds, make a diagonal cut just above a bud. The cut should slope down behind the bud.

Horizontal cut above a pair of buds

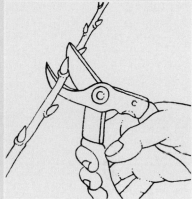

Diagonal cut above a single bud

sharp blades (*see* page 47). For thick branches, and pruning low down in the centre of the shrub or above head height, you might find it easier to use loppers.

When pruning, always make a nice, clean cut that will heal over effectively, preventing disease from getting into the branch. Do not tear the bark and leave shreds of it hanging that could cause dieback and further damage. Avoid 'snags'; these are bits of stem without growth buds that simply stay put

and eventually die back. They result when you do not prune just above a bud (*see* above).

Pruning deciduous shrubs

The main annual pruning session comes straight after flowering. In other words, shrubs that flower in early spring, such as forsythia, are pruned in late spring. Shrubs that flower in late spring, for instance lilac (*Syringa*), are pruned in early summer. Anything that flowers after late summer can be tidied up in autumn, and then pruned properly in late winter. This allows time for it to grow and produce flower buds through the next growing season.

Don't forget

Although it is good practice, you do not have to prune every year. If you miss a season, wait until the following year and prune after flowering rather than pruning at the wrong time of year for the shrub in question.

Shrubs that need minimal pruning

Acacia	Coronilla	Magnolia
Arbutus	Corylopsis	Mahonia
Berberis	Daphne	Pieris
Camellia	Escallonia	Prunus incisa
Choisya	Fothergilla	Rhododendron
Cistus	Hamamelis	Skimmia
Clethra	Hebe	Viburnum carlesii
Cornus kousa	Hibiscus	Viburnum plicatum

HOW TO prune early-flowering deciduous shrubs

Deciduous shrubs that flower in spring and early summer are best pruned straight after flowering, but need special attention when first planted. These include some *Buddleja*, *Chaenomeles*, *Deutzia*, *Kolkwitzia*, *Philadelphus*, *Ribes*, *Spiraea* and *Weigela*.

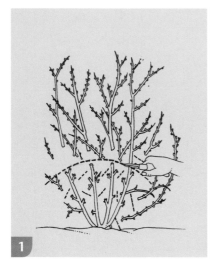

1

2

After planting, or in the first spring, shorten the main stems by two thirds and any lateral shoots to two or three buds to form a good framework. In the second spring, cut out any thin, weak shoots and overcrowded stems.

In subsequent years, immediately after flowering, cut out approximately one in five of the stems (usually the oldest) close to ground level. Shorten flowering shoots on the stronger-growing stems to two to four buds.

When to prune?

Basically, after flowering you cut out some of the stems that have flowered, allowing new shoots to develop from low down in the shrub. These will grow to produce the following season's main flowering stems.

This is very easy to see in the case of early-flowering shrubs such as flowering currants (*Ribes*), forsythias, deutzias and weigelas. The new shoots are already developing from the base of the stems and you cut back to these. You do not need to remove all flowered stems – just cut out some of the older ones and shorten others to maintain the shape and structure of the shrub.

Shrubs that flower in late summer and autumn, such as hydrangeas, buddleias, perovskias and caryopteris, are left until late winter before they are pruned. Most are best hard pruned at that stage,

Don't forget

There is not one main pruning season in the garden; it is done at various times of the year, according to the type of shrub. Avoid the tendency to go out and have one main hatchet pruning session. Although it will work for some things, it will be the wrong time for many others.

Suckering shrubs

Some shrubs have a habit of producing vigorous shoots from below ground or from the base of the plant. These suckers can be just part of the shrub's normal growth, as in the case of Christmas box (*Sarcococca*), in which case there won't be a problem. However, with grafted plants, such as some rhododendrons, the suckers are coming from the rootstock of the plant. Where this is the case, the vigorous shoots can become dominant and will eventually take over and replace the grafted cultivar.

Suckers usually show up as a vigorous shoot, or shoots, that grow up through the centre of the plant. These have a different habit, and usually different leaves, from the rest. As soon as you see a sucker growing from a rootstock, pull it out if you can, taking care not to damage the stem or root. If the sucker is too difficult to remove in this way, cut it off at the base, as close to the main stem as you can. Be aware that if you cut rather than pull the sucker, some dormant buds are more likely to remain at the base of the shoot to produce new suckers.

cutting back by two thirds to where new shoots are starting to appear on the lower part of the stems. Mophead and lacecap hydrangeas are treated more gently. The old flowerheads are removed back to pairs of fat buds and some of the old stems are cut back on mature plants.

Shrubs spoilt by pruning

Some of our loveliest deciduous shrubs are ruined by over-zealous pruning (see box, page 61). Witch hazel (*Hamamelis*), magnolias and hibiscus are best left alone as pruning spoils their natural shape. If you have to prune to restrict size, do it selectively. Remove whole branches, cutting right back into the plant, rather than trimming them, which would produce vigorous, stick-like growth on the ends of the branches.

This is the pruning method for those deciduous shrubs that flower after midsummer through autumn, and for trimming growth made during the earlier part of the season. This pruning would be carried out in late winter. Subjects pruned in this way include *Buddleja davidii*, *Caryopteris*, *Ceanothus* (deciduous), *Fuchsia*, *Hydrangea paniculata*, *Lavatera*, *Perovskia* and *Sambucus*.

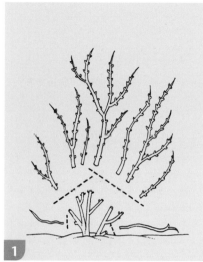
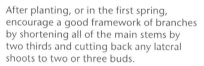

After planting, or in the first spring, encourage a good framework of branches by shortening all of the main stems by two thirds and cutting back any lateral shoots to two or three buds.

In the second spring, reduce the previous year's growth by about half its length. Remove any thin, weak, spindly shoots, and cut out one in three of any overcrowded shoots.

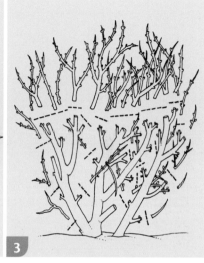

In subsequent years, completely remove any old or unproductive branches or stems to prevent overcrowding. Shorten the main stems by one third and cut back the lateral shoots to two or three buds.

Pruning evergreen shrubs

As a rule, evergreen shrubs require less in the way of annual pruning than deciduous ones. In the same way that they hang on to their leaves, they also like to hang on to their stems. Pruning is done to encourage denser, bushier growth and to prevent a straggly habit. It is also done to remove faded flowerheads and tidy the plant.

Some vigorous evergreens respond well to light pruning after flowering. For example, *Viburnum tinus* makes a nice, neat, mounded shrub if given a light prune in late spring, after flowering. This removes the faded flowers and reduces the spread of the shrub. Cut back the ends of the branches by about 20cm (8in) and the plant will soon respond with a flush of new growth.

Evergreen shrubs that can be trimmed

Viburnum tinus can also be trimmed with a pair of shears to produce a formal shape. The same is true of escallonia. It is tricky to know when to prune this one because it flowers all summer: trim it early in spring and it will flower on the new wood that grows as it matures. On a smaller scale, flowering shrubs like rock roses (*Helianthemum*) are best trimmed with shears after the flowers have faded. You can cut back the stems by half, or even a little more, to promote bushy plants.

Rhododendrons, azaleas and camellias

Compact rhododendrons and evergreen azaleas require no pruning, but can be cut back after flowering if the plants are straggly. Large-flowered rhododendrons also benefit from dead-heading. When the flowers have faded, you can usually break off the seedheads just above the top rosettes of leaves. This allows the new growth shoots to develop more quickly, which should lead to better flowering next season.

Camellias can also be pruned after flowering. This is best done from an early age if you want a compact plant of tidy or formal shape. However, bear in mind that some camellias have a much more arching, open habit and pruning does not improve them.

Usually secateurs are used for pruning but some shrubs, such as lavender, can be trimmed with shears. This is best done in late summer, straight after flowering.

To keep shrubs and trees in pots in tip-top condition, restrict their size and retain their shape, cut back all or some of the main branches by about one third. This should be carried out when repotting (*see* page 53).

Evergreen shrubs that need careful pruning

Some evergreen shrubs resent pruning, particularly as they mature. Young evergreen ceanothus, for example, can be lightly pruned to achieve bushy growth, but the plants resent hard pruning later in life and respond with sickly growth. The same is true of most sun roses (*Cistus*) and brooms (*Cytisus*). If you cut back into the bare wood behind the foliage at the ends of the branches, they will not normally produce new growth.

A good rule of thumb is to cut back only to where you can see growth buds or young shoots emerging from the woody stems. This is a useful guide when pruning lavenders, hebes and many grey-leaved shrubs, like cotton lavender (*Santolina*) and helichrysum. If you part the mound of foliage with your hands and peer into the centre, you will soon see if new shoots are present lower down in the shrub. They often are all at one level, making it easy to know where to cut.

Pruning lavenders

Lavenders should be pruned and dead-headed at the same time and, in this case, you can use a pair of hedge shears. As soon as the flowers fade in late summer, shear over the shrubs just below the base of the flower stems. The plants will produce a flush of new silver growth that will stay looking good all winter. If you don't get around to doing it in autumn, you can trim them in early spring, but this is not so good in a wet winter because the soggy flowers lie on the top of the plant and damage the foliage.

Rejuvenating old shrubs

Most gardeners face this problem at some point. You've inherited a large, overgrown shrub, or you have one in your garden that has just outgrown its beauty. All the flowers and leaves are on the top. They look good from the bedroom window, but when you're out enjoying the garden you look at bare, woody stems and sparse foliage. Do you get rid of it altogether, or do you give it a new lease of life?

Most vigorous deciduous and evergreen flowering shrubs respond well to the rejuvenation process, providing the plants are healthy and you can give them a little TLC after the secateurs and pruning saw have done their work. Some shrubs are particularly tolerant of hard pruning (*see* box, below). The rejuvenation process is usually quicker, and therefore more rewarding, with deciduous flowering shrubs.

Rejuvenation is not an overnight solution to the problem, and it can take two or three seasons to restore the shrub to its former beauty. It requires some patience. Before you embark on the process, you need to decide if you can live in the meantime with the shrub in its less-than-beautiful state. If you can, then obviously you are preserving valuable maturity and structure in your garden, and a new specimen would probably take longer than the rejuvenation process to reach these proportions anyway. However, some shrubs are short-lived and are therefore not worth attempting to rejuvenate (*see* box, bottom).

Shrubs that tolerate hard pruning

Berberis darwinii	Philadelphus
Callistemon	Prunus laurocerasus
Choisya	Rhododendron (hardy hybrids)
Deutzia	
Escallonia	Rosmarinus
Hebe	Syringa
Kolkwitzia	Viburnum tinus
Mahonia	Weigela
Olearia	

Shrubs to replace rather than renovate

Abutilon	Cytisus
Ceanothus	Lavandula
Cistus	Lavatera

HOW TO renovate a shrub

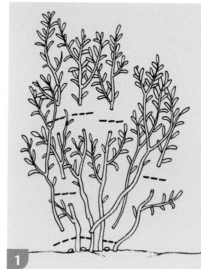

1 In late winter or early spring, cut up to half of the main stems to the base or to a low framework, concentrating on badly placed, old, and diseased wood. Shorten the rest by up to half their length. The aim is encourage growth from the base.

2 The following year, cut back half of the remaining main stems to ground level or the low framework. Thin the new shoots that formed as a result of pruning in Step 1. Leave the strongest shoots on the remains of the thickest stubs to form a new shrub.

3 In the third year, cut any remaining old stems that have produced either no new stems or only thin, weak growths down to soil level.

4 Further growths may appear from the old stumps from time to time for several years. Prune these out, or pull them away if you spot them while they are still soft.

Growing a flowering shrub as a standard

Some shrubs can be trained to create a totally different effect from the natural habit of the plant; you need to start with a young plant, before its branch framework develops. You also need to give the plant regular attention to keep it in shape. The results are striking, especially when shrubs grown as standards are in bloom.

Other shrubs suitable for creating a standard

Hibiscus syriacus
Hydrangea paniculata
Lavandula angustifolia
Rosmarinus officinalis
Syringa vulgaris

To keep a fuchsia flowering, cut back the previous year's growth when new shoots emerge in spring and dead-head regularly.

A standard fuchsia is the perfect example and is a good practice plant as it is fast-growing, showing you success in a year or two. It makes an excellent subject for a patio container in a sheltered site and can also be used as a focal point in a bed or border. Standard shrubs give a formal effect and suit town gardens.

Creating a standard

To create a standard, strip sideshoots off a cutting or young plant to leave only a main stem. Transfer it to a 10cm (4in) pot to grow on and push in a short houseplant cane beside it as support. Tie in the lengthening stem to the cane. Remove shoots that appear along the lower part of the stem. When the pot is filled with roots and the stem has reached the top of the cane, repot into a 15cm (6in) pot. Replace the houseplant cane with a bamboo cane, and leave the plant to grow on as before. When the stem has reached the top of the cane, pinch out the growing-tip. Remove any sideshoots on the clear stem, but let those that form just below the tip grow to about 5cm (2in), then pinch them out. From now on, just keep pinching out the tips of those shoots when the new sideshoots reach about 5cm (2in), building up a large, dense, spherical head. When it is large enough, stop pinching, and your standard will flower at the usual time.

HOW TO create a standard

1 Remove all sideshoots from the young plant or rooted cutting, allowing only the main stem to extend. Transfer the plant to a slightly larger pot to grow on.

2 Tie the stem to a 1m (3ft) cane for support and to create an upright habit. When the shoot reaches beyond the top of the cane, stop it by pinching out the growing-tip.

3 Keep pinching out the tips of the shoots at the top of the plant when the sideshoots reach about 5cm (2in) long; the head will slowly grow larger and denser.

Propagation

You can make more of your flowering shrubs by practising a little propagation: taking cuttings, layering or even sowing seed. Whether you want more of the same shrub or not, there is something satisfying about propagating plants. Not only are you getting more shrubs for free, but you're proving your gardening skills.

Why propagate?

If there is a plant that you particularly like, and is admired by others, it is very satisfying to have a young specimen that you can pass on to a fellow gardener. Also, some shrubs are short-lived; if you can start new plants from cuttings, you will have replacements waiting in the wings to take over if the original one dies. If you're moving house, it is not good practice to dig up your shrubs and take them with you. Instead, it's much better to take cuttings or layers and plant your new garden with those. Home propagation is also an excellent way to bulk up your plant stock, particularly of those good garden basics that hold a flowering-shrub planting scheme together.

Taking cuttings

Taking cuttings is the commonest method of propagating flowering shrubs. Some root easily, some do not, and there are different ways of doing it. Basically, you're taking a piece of stem, perhaps with leaves, and encouraging it to grow roots.

HOW TO take hardwood cuttings

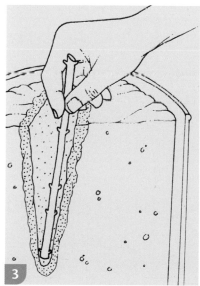
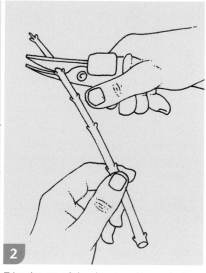
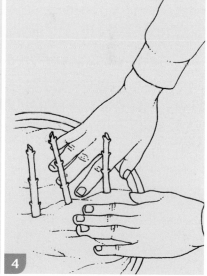
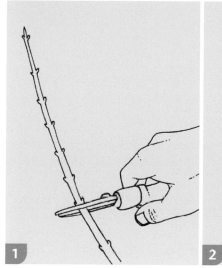

1 Using secateurs, remove a length of healthy stem from the current year's growth. Make a straight cut. If there are sideshoots present, trim them off.

2 Trim the top of the shoot, making a sloping cut just above a bud. The cutting should be about 20cm (8in) long. It may help to dip the base in hormone rooting powder or gel.

3 Fill a pot with free-draining cutting compost and moisten the compost well. Make a small slit trench in the compost. Insert the cutting into the trench, base first, leaving only the top third of the cutting showing above the surface.

4 Continue inserting cuttings, then close the trench by firming compost around it. Water well and stand the pot in a well-lit, frost-free, sheltered spot outside over winter. Once the cuttings have rooted, pot them up separately.

Remember that you need to keep this plant alive if it's going to grow roots and make a new plant. Hygiene is important, so always use clean tools and pots and fresh compost, and make sure the knife or secateurs that you use to take the cutting are sharp. Use healthy plant material and, if you can, always take more cuttings than you need. If you take three cuttings none will root; if you take 20 they all will – that's gardening for you!

Hardwood cuttings

This type of cutting is used to propagate deciduous shrubs. Vigorous subjects, such as flowering currants (*Ribes*) and forsythia, root easily by this method (*see* page 67). Hardwood cuttings are taken in early winter, when the leaves have fallen. The advantage of taking a hardwood cutting is that it doesn't have leaves to support and can therefore concentrate on producing roots. Also, because the cutting is woody, it doesn't dry out too quickly.

Choose straight shoots and cut about 25–30cm (10–12in) from the end of the shoot. Trim off the top and plunge the cutting into a deep pot of well-drained cutting compost or a mixture of John Innes No. 1 and horticultural grit. You can then stand the pot outside in a sheltered spot or in a cold frame. Do not place it in a warm environment; if you do, it will be the leaf buds that develop, rather than the roots.

Be patient – root formation can take several weeks. If you pull the cuttings out to take a look, you'll break off those young roots as they start to form.

HOW TO take semi-ripe cuttings

1 Take a cutting about 10cm (4in) long that is green near the tips and woodier where it meets the main stem. If it is a sideshoot, pull it off the main stem at the heel (shown above). If it is a stem-tip cutting, cut it about 10cm (4in) from the stem-tip, just behind a leaf node (*see* box, opposite).

2 Using a sharp knife or secateurs, remove the lower leaves from the bottom half to two thirds of the stem. Pinch out the tip of the shoot and carefully remove any thorns that may be present on the stem. Trim the heel neatly to remove any torn pieces of bark.

3 You can dip the cut end of the cutting in hormone rooting powder or gel (but you don't have to; it may just help some plants to root). Insert the cuttings around the edge of a pot filled with moist cutting compost or multipurpose compost, taking care not to damage them.

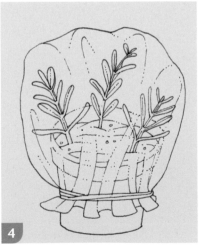

4 Water the pot thoroughly and stand it in a sheltered corner of the garden or in a cold frame until the cuttings have rooted the following spring. Smaller semi-ripe cuttings may root more easily if covered with a plastic bag, as long as they are not in a hot position where they can dry out.

Taking a stem-tip cutting

A cutting is a short piece of stem with leaves and growth buds. It is cut in different ways according to the plant that you are planning to propagate. Some cuttings, particularly semi-ripe ones, can be taken by pulling a sideshoot away from the main shoot with a small 'heel' of bark still attached (*see* step 1, opposite). Alternatively, they can be taken from the tip of the stem by trimming just beneath a node or leaf-joint, shown below.

NODAL CUTTING
Cuttings of flowering shrubs are frequently taken by cutting the stem straight across immediately below a node – that is where a leaf or a pair of leaves joins on to the main stem. The leaves nearest to the cut are removed when the cutting is prepared.

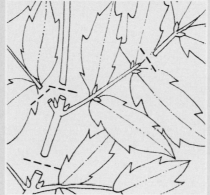

LEAF-BUD CUTTING
This type of cutting is taken to propagate some shrubs, especially mahonias. The stem is cut into sections immediately above one set of leaves, and again above the next. The leaves are reduced in number and size, and the cutting is pushed into the compost so that the tip of the stem and buds are just above the surface.

about 12cm (5in) long. They are taken immediately below a leaf node (*see* box, left). They wilt easily, so you need to preserve their moisture using a propagator cover or plastic bag. However, if they are going to root, they do so quickly. As they will have to support leaves, it's common to cut off half of each leaf to reduce the amount of water loss. Prepare and plant them in the same way as semi-ripe cuttings (*see* opposite).

The soft, fleshy new growth of many deciduous shrubs can be used as softwood cuttings: abutilons, deutzias, fuchsias, hydrangeas and mock orange (*Philadelphus*) are a few examples of flowering shrubs that can be propagated in this way.

Semi-ripe cuttings

This type of cutting is used for both deciduous and evergreen shrubs and is usually taken in late summer or early autumn, when the current year's growth has just started to turn woody. The cuttings are often taken at a heel (*see* opposite); that is where a sideshoot meets the main stem. It's a good idea to pinch out the tip of the shoot if it's soft, otherwise it's likely to wilt anyway. Cuttings are inserted into pots of well-drained compost, so that about one third of the stem sits below the surface. The compost needs to be kept moist and the pots should be kept out of direct sunlight in a cold frame, unheated greenhouse or a sheltered, shady corner of the garden. The cuttings should have rooted, ready for potting on, by the following spring.

A good test to see if the sideshoots of the shrub are in the right condition for taking cuttings is to wrap one around your finger. If the shoot wraps around without breaking it is still soft enough and at the right stage for propagation.

Softwood cuttings

These are the cuttings made from the soft, new growth shoots of deciduous or evergreen shrubs that usually appear in spring, but can be produced by some shrubs at any stage in the growing season. Cuttings are soft, fleshy and usually

Flowering currants (*Ribes*) are propagated by semi-ripe cuttings in late summer or early autumn. Stand the tray in a cold frame until the cuttings root (usually by late spring).

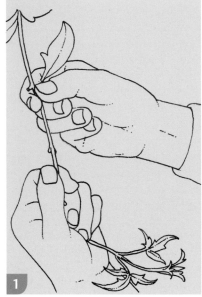

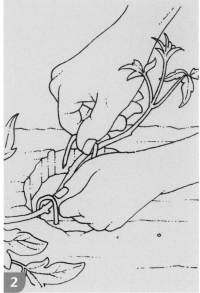

1

Select a strong and healthy, pliable, low-growing shoot and strip off leaves about 20cm (8in) behind the growing-tip.

2

Pull the shoot down to ground level and bend it at right angles, pegging it down into a shallow hole.

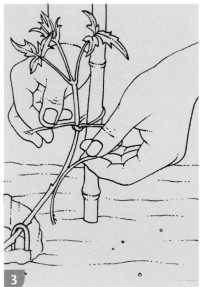

3

About 20cm (8in) of the shoot should protrude and be tied to a short bamboo cane so that it is held vertically out of the hole.

4

Fill in the hole and firm before watering thoroughly. Wait for the shoot to produce roots (the time it takes varies according to variety) and then cut off the new plant.

Layering

This is a great way to grow one or two new shrubs from an existing plant, particularly with shrubs with low branches that can be anchored to the ground. Rather than separating the cutting from the original plant you keep it attached, on a sort of life-support machine. Basically, you choose a branch as a cutting, bury part of it in the ground and wait for it to produce roots. You then separate the new plant from its parent by cutting the stem that connects them once the young plant can fend for itself. Shrubs to propagate by layering include some heathers (*Calluna*), *Magnolia*, *Kolkwitzia* and *Leycesteria*, but virtually anything is worth a go.

Sowing seed

Although many flowering shrubs can set seed, few are propagated in this way. Seed produces prolific offspring, meaning wastage is high. Also, offspring raised from seed can vary from the parent plant – grow them from cuttings, and they will be identical to the parent. However, seed is useful as a means of propagating brooms (*Cytisus*), *Lupinus arboreus* and *Colutea*, all members of the pea family.

Grafting

This is really a job for the professional nurseryman or highly experienced gardener. Basically, a cutting (a scion) is taken from the plant you want to propagate and it is grafted onto the roots and a bit of stem (the stock) of another similar, but easier-to-grow plant. You can tell if a plant has been grafted because there is usually a clear ridge or bump on the stem just above soil level.

How and when to propagate flowering shrubs

KEY: S = SOFTWOOD CUTTINGS, SR = SEMI-RIPE CUTTINGS, H = HARDWOOD CUTTINGS, L = LAYERING * Often best raised from seed

SHRUB	S	SR	H	L	TRICKY	BEST SEASON	SHRUB	S	SR	H	L	TRICKY	BEST SEASON
Abelia	x			x		summer	× Halimiocistus		x				summer
Abeliophyllum	x	x		x		early summer/autumn	Hamamelis			x	x		autumn
Abutilon	x	x			x (some)	late summer	Hebe		x				late summer
Andromeda		x				summer	Helianthemum		x				midsummer
Arctostaphylos		x		x		summer/autumn	Hibiscus		x			x	late summer
Berberis		x				late summer	Hydrangea	x	x				early/late summer
Brachyglottis		x	x			midsummer/autumn	Hypericum	x	x				early/late summer
Buddleja		x	x			early summer/winter	Indigofera	x					early/midsummer
Bupleurum		x		x		midsummer	Itea		x				mid/late summer
Callistemon *		x				late summer	Jasminum		x		x		summer/autumn
Calluna		x				midsummer	Kalmia		x		x	x	late summer/autumn
Camellia		x	x	x		summer/autumn	Kerria		x		x		summer/autumn
Caragana *	x					late spring	Kolkwitzia		x				summer
Carpenteria	x			x		summer/winter	Lavandula	x	x				spring/late summer
Caryopteris		x				summer/winter	Lavatera	x					spring/summer
Ceanothus	x	x				summer	Leucothoe		x		x		late summer/autumn
Ceratostigma		x				summer	Leycesteria			x		x	autumn
Chaenomeles		x		x		early summer	Lonicera		x	x			late summer/autumn
Chimonanthus			x	x		summer	Magnolia	x	x			x	early summer/autumn
Choisya	x	x				summer	Mahonia		x				early/midsummer
Cistus	x					summer	Myrtus		x				early/midsummer
Clerodendrum		x				summer	Olearia		x				late summer/autumn
Clethra	x			x		early summer/autumn	Osmanthus		x				summer
Convolvulus		x				summer	Paeonia		x				summer
Corokia		x				autumn	Philadelphus	x	x				summer
Coronilla						summer	Phlomis	x	x				summer/autumn
Corylopsis	x			x	x	autumn	Phygelius	x					mid/late summer
Cotoneaster *		x		x		summer	Pieris		x		x		late summer/autumn
Cytisus *		x				midsummer	Potentilla		x				late summer
Daboecia		x				summer	Rhododendron		x		x	x (some)	summer
Daphne		x			x (some)	summer	Ribes		x	x			autumn
Desfontainia		x				autumn	Rosmarinus		x				mid/late summer
Deutzia	x	x	x			early summer/autumn	Salix		x	x			summer/autumn
Diervilla		x				summer	Sambucus		x	x			late summer/winter
Dipelta		x	x			summer/autumn	Santolina		x				mid/late summer
Erica		x				summer	Sarcococca		x				autumn
Escallonia		x				summer	Skimmia		x				late summer/autumn
Exochorda	x			x		early summer	Sophora		SR				autumn
Fabiana		x				summer	Sorbaria		x				autumn
Fatsia		x				summer	Spartium *					x	late summer
Forsythia		x	x			summer/autumn	Spiraea		x				late summer
Fothergilla		x		x		autumn	Syringa	x	x	x			late spring/autumn
Fremontodendron		x				summer	Teucrium		x				mid/late summer
Fuchsia	x					anytime	Thymus		x				early summer
Garrya		x				summer	Ulex *		x				late summer
Gaultheria		x				summer	Viburnum	x	x				early/midsummer
Genista *		x				late summer	Weigela	x	x	x			early summer/autumn

Plant problems and remedies

Flowering shrubs suffer from a similar range of pests and diseases as other groups of popular garden plants. You can go a long way to avoiding problems by growing the right plants in the right situation and by making sure they remain healthy and vigorous. A strong-growing, contented specimen is more likely to shrug off problems without the need for intervention.

To prevent problems in the first place, it makes sense to practise good garden hygiene – a garden doesn't have to be tidy, but it should be well kept. Also, try to stay vigilant. If pest or disease outbreaks are caught early, they're easier to treat and the shrubs will suffer less damage in the long run.

Controlling pests

Check your flowering shrubs regularly for signs of damage or disease. All it takes is a walk around the garden of an evening. Individual pests, such as caterpillars, can be picked off, and small colonies of sap-sucking insects, found in the soft growing-tips of plants, are easy to rub out between finger and thumb. Removing by hand is often the simplest remedy.

Another one of the most effective ways of controlling pests is to encourage natural predators that feed on them. You can do this by providing suitable habitats where they can feed, breed and set up home. Nectar-rich flowers, for example, will attract hoverflies and lacewings that eat aphids, spider mite and other insect pests, while logs provide a home for ground beetles and centipedes that devour rootfly and vine weevils.

If you must use chemicals, choose less invasive, selective treatments that tackle just the pest in question.

Aphids

These attack and colonize growing-tips. They suck sap, weakening the host, and excrete sticky honeydew that often becomes colonized by black sooty mould, which makes it harder for the shrub to photosynthesize.

Prevention and control Squash small colonies by hand. Encourage natural predators such as lacewings. Treat large colonies with an organic control, such as insecticidal soap.

Capsid bugs

Leaves at the shoot-tips might become distorted, with small holes, when attacked by these sap-sucking pests. Flowers can be damaged in a similar way.

Prevention and control Keep your borders well weeded and spray problem plants with insecticide.

Caterpillars

These are the larvae of the butterflies and moths that feed on flowering shrubs. Signs of attack are usually irregular holes eaten in the leaves.

Prevention and control Pick off and squash caterpillars, or cut out stems and branches where caterpillars are feeding. For severe infestations, spray on a biological control to limit their spread.

Flea beetles

Plant leaves riddled with tiny pinprick holes indicate flea-beetle damage. The beetles particularly like fuchsias and become active during dry spells in spring.

Prevention and control Remove damaged foliage, and feed and water all plants in dry spells to encourage healthy growth.

Galls

Many fly and wasp larvae as well as mites cause galls to develop on flowering shrubs such as *Camellia* and *Forsythia*. The galls are swollen structures produced by the plant in response to chemicals secreted by the larvae. Plant growth and development are not affected.

Prevention and control They have no harmful effect on the plant so control measures are unnecessary.

Eelworms

Flowering shrubs, including weigelas, are prone to leaf and bud attack from eelworms. These are microscopic nematode worms,

which are invisible to the naked eye, that feed within their host plants, causing damage.

Prevention and control Remove virus-infected plants from the garden and do not replant with the same types of plant, otherwise they may quickly be infected by the eelworms. Not all eelworms are pests; some of them are used to control slugs.

Leaf miners

The grubs of these tiny flies create 'tunnels' as they feed within the plant's leaves, creating characteristic, maze-like patterns. Damage is common on *Pyracantha*, *Polygonum* and lilacs (*Syringa*). If plants are healthy they can tolerate attacks. Damage tends to be unsightly rather than harmful.
Prevention and control Remove and destroy damaged leaves.

Red spider mite

Buddleja, *Fuchsia*, *Hydrangea*, *Jasminum* and *Choisya* can all fall victim to this common pest, particularly during warm weather in sheltered parts of the garden. Signs of red spider mite are stunted growth, and curled and mottled leaves covered with a fine webbing that protects breeding colonies.
Prevention and control Red spider mite prefers dry conditions, so water

plants to maintain high humidity. Use a biological control or spray with insecticide when any signs of damage appear.

Scale insects

These sap-feeding pests cause stunted growth and yellowing of the leaves. The most problematic for flowering shrubs are cushion scale  (*Camellia*), muscle scale (*Ceanothus*, *Cornus* and *Cotoneaster*), brown scale (*Chaenomeles*, *Escallonia*, *Rosmarinus* and *Weigela*), horse chestnut scale (*Cornus*, *Skimmia* and *Magnolia*), hydrangea scale and viburnum scale. Plants are weakened by the feeding scales, leaves may fall and growth is inhibited.
Prevention and control Check new plants to avoid introducing scale insects to your garden. Isolated scales can be picked off or pruned out. Apply a biological control to limit numbers. Severe infestations can be controlled by spraying with a systemic insecticide in early summer.

Slugs and snails

Signs of slug and snail damage include chewed leaves and stripped foliage. They enjoy *Choisya* and *Yucca*.
Prevention and control Protect vulnerable young shrubs with barriers of grit,

copper collars and beer traps. Pick off the pests by torchlight. You can also use a biological control, containing nematodes, in the surrounding soil.

Thrips

These elongated insects feed in large numbers on the upper side of leaves and on flowers and buds of many plants, including lilacs. They cause a characteristic silvery mottling and some distortion to plant parts.
Prevention and control Keep plants well watered and spray with an organic pesticide.

Vine weevils

This pest is now endemic in the UK, particularly in the mild south-east. They are especially troublesome on *Camellia*, *Hydrangea*, *Rhododendron* and *Skimmia*, but also attack other shrubs. This destructive pest disfigures foliage and destroys roots. The cream-coloured, brown-headed grubs feed unseen on roots, while the adults munch notches out of the edges of leaves.
Prevention and control Collect up adults at night by torchlight to prevent them from breeding. Encourage predators such as birds, frogs, toads, hedgehogs and ground beetles. For severe infestations, use a nematode-based biological control.

Common diseases

Diseases are caused by bacteria, fungi and viruses. Fungi and bacteria are encouraged by poor weather conditions, while viruses are often carried by insect pests. All problems are exacerbated by poor husbandry. As with garden pests, the best way of tackling diseases is prevention. Keeping your plants healthy, and giving them the site, soil and aspect they prefer, will help them fight off common diseases. When buying new shrubs, try to choose disease-resistant varieties.

Botrytis

Also known as grey mould, this common fungus attacks many shrubs and results in yellowing and browning of the leaves. The upper parts of the stem may die and fungal spores develop on decaying plant material. It usually takes hold after pest damage to flowers or fruits.

Prevention and control Prune out affected stems and burn them. Also maintain good air circulation and hygiene. Dead-head plants regularly.

Coral spot

Individual branches of shrubs, such as *Ribes* or *Magnolia,* are prone to this fungal disease, which causes pink or reddish-orange spots on old or dead stems of woody plants. The fungus can spread quite easily from dead wood to healthy growth.

Prevention and control Prune to remove affected wood and burn infected material straight away.

Downy mildew

Yellow patches appear on upper leaf surfaces with corresponding patches of mould beneath in damp weather. Large areas of the leaf might be infected and the leaves might die, but the plant itself might not be severely infected. Hebes are particularly vulnerable to this disease.

Prevention and control The disease is most common in damp and humid growing situations. Avoid overcrowding and maintain good air circulation around established shrubs by careful pruning.

Fireblight

Young shoots of flowering shrubs, including *Amelanchier* and *Cotoneaster,* are prone to this bacterial disease, which causes the shoots to blacken and shrivel as if scorched. It eventually kills off the entire plant.

Prevention and control Remove and burn any stems showing signs of fireblight. Grow varieties resistant to it as there is no chemical control.

Honey fungus

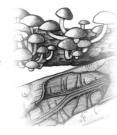

Many shrubs are susceptible to honey fungus, with *Cotoneaster*, *Ribes* and *Syringa* being some of the more vulnerable. Initial symptoms include dying back of leafy branches or failure of leaves to appear in spring. Death can be rapid or can take several years. Signs of infection can be found by peeling back the bark where thin sheets of creamy fungal growth, smelling of mushrooms, will be found. Also, black bootlace-like growths are visible under the bark and in the soil. Honey-coloured toadstools might also appear.

Prevention and control Plants growing strongly are less vulnerable. Remove infected plants with as much root as possible. Choose plants with some resistance, such as *Chaenomeles* and *Hebe.*

Leaf spots

This disease is characterized by discoloured, rounded spots that can merge together to affect large parts of the leaf, which might turn brown and fall off. Leaf spot can infect a wide range of flowering shrubs, such as *Camellia*, especially those struggling in poor conditions. Attacks are seldom very serious, so don't warrant treatment.

Prevention and control Clear up and dispose of infected leaves of deciduous shrubs before new foliage appears in spring. Mulching will also help prevent spores in the soil infecting new foliage.

Powdery mildew

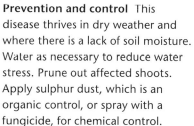

A white, powdery-like coating might appear on almost any part of the plant. Growth can become stunted and in severe attacks the plant may die.

Prevention and control This disease thrives in dry weather and where there is a lack of soil moisture. Water as necessary to reduce water stress. Prune out affected shoots. Apply sulphur dust, which is an organic control, or spray with a fungicide, for chemical control.

Rust

The upper surface of the leaves has yellow blotches while the underside is covered in rust-coloured spots; leaves eventually drop off. This fungal disease affects many popular flowering shrubs, including *Berberis*, *Ribes*, *Fuchsia*, *Hypericum*, *Lavatera*, *Mahonia* and *Rhododendron*.

Prevention and control Regular pruning will prevent overcrowding of mature stems and increase air circulation between plants, thereby limiting the spread of this fungal disease. Remove any leaves infected by rust and take them off site or burn them rather than adding them to the compost heap.

Cucumber mosaic virus

Daphne and several other flowering shrubs are prone to this virus, which is primarily spread by aphids. It can also be spread by handling diseased plants, and by using contaminated tools. The virus causes mottling or mosaic patterns and distortion of the leaves. Plants might die.

Prevention and control Grow resistant cultivars. Remove the infected plants and burn as soon as symptons are identified. There is no cure.

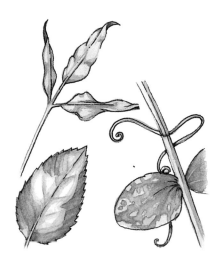

Other problems that affect flowering shrubs

BIRD AND INSECT DAMAGE

Keep an eye out for anything that interferes with the flowering performance or display of flowering shrubs. Bullfinches, for example, can target the brilliant yellow blooms of *Forsythia* during the spring. Earwigs may be a problem on *Buddleja*.

DROUGHT AND WATERLOGGING

During the summer, drought can be a particular issue for *Ceanothus* and *Hydrangea*, while on heavier soils the roots of broom (*Cytisus*) are particularly vulnerable to waterlogging.

FROST DAMAGE

Environmental troubles, such as bad weather, are often more of an issue with flowering shrubs. All not-so-hardy shrubs, such as rosemary (*Rosmarinus*), are at risk during really cold and frosty conditions unless they are well protected (*see* page 59). Even some otherwise hardy flowering shrubs, such as broom (*Cytisus*), *Ceanothus*, *Hydrangea*, Mexican orange blossom (*Choisya*), *Magnolia* and *Rhododendron*, can find an unexpectedly late frost singeing their delicate blooms or tender new growth.

IRON AND MAGNESIUM DEFICIENCY

Chalky soils can cause flowering shrubs such as *Ceanothus*, *Hydrangea*, flowering quince (*Chaenomeles*), *Rhododendron*, *Skimmia*, *Magnolia* and flowering currants (*Ribes*) to suffer from iron deficiency resulting in lime-induced chlorosis, while *Hydrangea* and *Skimmia* are prone to magnesium deficiency on some soils. Leaves turn pale yellow. Feed with iron or magnesium compounds.

VIRUSES

Signs of virus attack are usually stunted or distorted growth and yellowing or white-streaked leaves. Remove and burn affected plants immediately; clear away weeds and disinfect tools, as these may harbour viruses. Keep potential carriers, such as aphids, under control (*see* page 72). If possible, always buy certified virus-free plants.

SOIL-BORNE PATHOGENS

Verticillium wilt affects *Berberis*, *Cotinus* and *Daphne*; plants will deteriorate and may die (look for longitudinal brown stripes beneath the bark). Phytophthora affects heathers (*Calluna*), *Camellia*, *Cornus*, *Rhododendron*, flowering currants (*Ribes*) and *Skimmia*; the foliage becomes sparse and chlorotic, affected roots usually turn black and plants may be killed. Unfortunately, there is nothing you can do about these two problems apart from dispose of the affected plants and the soil around their roots and start again; improving soil drainage will help prevent phytophthora spreading. (*See also* Honey fungus, opposite.)

Recommended flowering shrubs

While there are countless shrubs that are valued primarily for their attractive leaves, stems or habit, there are many that are distinguished by the beauty and fragrance of their flowers and – in many cases – the brightly coloured fruit that follows them. In this section of the book, you'll find a wealth of flowering shrubs to choose from, including old favourites as well as other, more unusual varieties. There are beautiful shrubs for every season, so with a little forward planning you'll be able to enjoy splashes of colour and sweet scents in your garden throughout the year, even in winter.

A–Z directory

Before choosing a shrub, it's always worth doing your homework: familiarize yourself with your garden soil and aspect (*see* pages 48–9) and select plants that will thrive in those conditions. There are flowering shrubs to suit every situation and soil type.

The directory that follows illustrates a wide range of shrubs grown mainly for their flowers. It does not include most of the large, tree-like shrubs (featured on pages 26–7), smaller, woody-based sub-shrubs (*see* page 25) or roses. For flowering shrubs that need to be trained against a wall, *see* Climbers and Wall Shrubs in the same series. For other recommendations, *see* Plants for a purpose, pages 43–5.

KEY to symbols

In this chapter the following symbols are used to indicate a plant's preferred growing conditions. A rough idea is also given as to what each plant's height (H) and spread (S) might be at maturity. *Unless otherwise specified, plants are fully hardy and deciduous.*

○   Prefers/tolerates an open, sunny site

◐   Prefers/tolerates some shade

●   Prefers/tolerates full shade

❄   Will survive winter in a sheltered site

❀   Always needs protection from frost

◗   Prefers/tolerates moist soil

◌   Prefers/tolerates dry soil

⇊   Needs well-drained soil

pH↓   Needs/prefers acidic soil

pH↑   Needs/prefers alkaline soil

pH→   Needs/prefers neutral soil

❦   Needs humus-rich soil

❖   Season of main interest (e.g. flowers, foliage, stems, berries)

Abelia × grandiflora 'Francis Mason'
○ ❄ ⇊ ❖ MIDSUMMER to AUTUMN
H 1.5m (5ft) S 2m (6ft)

This well-behaved variety bears fragrant, pinkish-white, trumpet-shaped flowers on arching stems from midsummer to mid-autumn. The semi-evergreen foliage is yellow with dark green blotches. In colder areas grow it among other shrubs or against a sheltered wall for protection.

Abeliophyllum distichum
White forsythia
○ ❄ ⇊ ❖ LATE WINTER to EARLY SPRING
H and S 1.5m (5ft)

Masses of tiny, white or pinkish-white scented flowers appear in late winter on bare, purple-tinged stems. It is an attractive multi-stemmed shrub, ideal for a sheltered border in full sun. Cut stems for late-winter arrangements indoors. Good variety: Roseum Group.

Abutilon 'Kentish Belle'
Chinese lantern
○ ❄ ⇊ ❖ SUMMER to AUTUMN
H and S 2.5m (8ft)

This is a graceful, evergreen shrub that bears stunning, bell-shaped, pale yellow flowers, burnt orange at the base, on purplish arching stems. It is ideal for growing in containers in colder areas and, elsewhere, can be grown against a sheltered wall or fence if it is protected during severe winter weather.

Abutilon megapotamicum
Trailing abutilon
○ ❄ ⇊ ❖ SUMMER to AUTUMN
H and S 2m (6ft)

A delightfully lax, evergreen shrub with eye-catching red and yellow lanterns, this is an unusual plant for a patio pot or a cool conservatory. In milder areas, if protected during severe winter weather, it will add a tropical look to a sheltered wall or fence. Wall training also shows off the flowers well. Good variety: 'Variegatum' (yellow-mottled leaves).

Andromeda polifolia
Bog rosemary, Marsh andromeda
○ ◑ ◌ pH↓ ✦ ❖SPRING to EARLY SUMMER
H 40cm (16in) S 60cm (2ft)

Clusters of small, white or pink, pitcher-shaped flowers adorn this shrub in spring and summer. It is low-growing and semi-evergreen, with narrow, silvery-green leaves, and fits well with other acid-loving plants in a woodland area. Good varieties: 'Alba' (white flowers; H 15cm/6in, S 20cm/8in); 'Compacta' (pink flowers; H and S 20cm/8in; shown above).

Arctostaphylos uva-ursi
Common bearberry
○ ◑ ◌ ↕↕ pH↓ ❖SPRING to EARLY SUMMER, AUTUMN
H 10cm (4in) S 50cm (20in)

A useful mat-forming, evergreen shrub, this makes unusual ground cover on a sunny bank with acid soil or under other acid-loving plants such as azaleas and rhododendrons. In late spring and early summer pretty, pink-tinted white flowers, which turn to red berries in autumn, nestle in the leathery, dark green foliage.

Azalea *see* Rhododendron

Berberis darwinii Barberry
○ ◑ ↕↕ ❖LATE SPRING, AUTUMN
H and S 3m (10ft)

This splendid, spiny, evergreen barberry bears loose clusters of burnt-orange flowers in late spring and rounded, blue-purple berries in autumn. Vigorous and easy to grow in sun or semi-shade, it has holly-like, prickly foliage, making an impenetrable flowering hedge.

Berberis thunbergii Barberry
○ ◑ ↕↕ ❖LATE SPRING, AUTUMN
H 1m (40in) S 2.5m (8ft)

Yellow, red-tinged flowers in late spring are followed in autumn by red fruits as the bright green deciduous leaves turn fiery shades (shown above). Easy to grow, this shrub makes a fine informal hedge or filler plant. Compact forms do well in pots. Good varieties: 'Aurea' (yellow leaves; H 60cm/2ft, S 75cm/30in); f. *atropurpurea* 'Bagatelle' (more compact and low-growing, with dark red-purple leaves; H 30cm/12in, S 40cm/16in); f.a. 'Dart's Red Lady' (purple leaves; H 1m/40in, S 2.5m/8ft); f.a. 'Helmond Pillar' (narrowly upright, with rich red-purple leaves; H 1.5m/5ft, S 60cm/2ft).

Berberis verruculosa Barberry
○ ◑ ↕↕ ❖EARLY SUMMER, AUTUMN
H and S 1.5m (5ft)

A useful, compact, evergreen shrub, this barberry has spine-tipped leaves on warty stems that bear solitary, golden, early-summer flowers on arching shoots. The flowers are followed by shiny purple fruits. Vigorous and easy to grow, this berberis makes a neat specimen shrub for partially shaded areas.

Brachyglottis (Dunedin Group) 'Sunshine'
○ ↕↕ ❖EARLY SUMMER
H 1.5m (5ft) S 2m (6ft)

Formerly known as *Senecio*, this cheery evergreen shrub produces charming, sunny-yellow, daisy-like flowers *en masse* in early summer over a mound of strokeable, furry, silvery foliage. It is ideal as a filler in a sunny border and, being wind- and salt-tolerant, a good choice for exposed and coastal gardens.

Buddleja alternifolia
○ ⁂ ❖ EARLY SUMMER, AUTUMN
H and S 4m (13ft)

Dramatic, stiffly arching branches are wreathed throughout early summer in dense clusters of fragrant, lilac flowers busy with butterflies and bees. This buddleia can look most effective trained as a standard, with stems gracefully cascading. Autumn tints are a bonus.

Buddleja davidii 'Black Knight'
Butterfly bush
○ ⁂ ❖ SUMMER, AUTUMN
H 3m (10ft) S 5m (16ft)

Great for beginners, this easy-to-grow shrub bears dense spikes of nectar-rich, fragrant, dark purple flowers in summer, a magnet for butterflies and bees. It has butter-yellow autumn tints. Other good varieties: 'Harlequin' (reddish-purple flowers, cream-edged leaves); 'Nanho Blue' (lilac-blue flowers); 'Nanho Purple' (violet-blue flowers); 'Pink Delight' (pink flowers); 'Royal Red' (red-purple flowers); 'White Profusion' (white flowers).

Buddleja globosa Orange ball tree
○ ❄ ⁂ ❖ EARLY SUMMER
H and S 5m (16ft)

This attractive and unusual, rounded, semi-evergreen shrub with deeply veined, dark green leaves is decorated in early summer with eye-catching bright yellow to dark orange balls of fragrant flowers. It is ideal for growing at the back of a sunny border.

Buddleja 'Lochinch'
○ ⁂ ❖ LATE SUMMER to EARLY AUTUMN
H 2.5m (8ft) S 3m (10ft)

The lax, arching branches of this elegant shrub carry large clusters of tiny, nectar-rich, honey-scented, violet-blue flowers, each with an orange eye. Flowering from late summer until early autumn, it makes a big impact in a sunny border, where it will attract the attention of butterflies, bees and other beneficial insects.

Bupleurum fruticosum
Shrubby hare's ear
○ ❄ ⁂ ❖ MIDSUMMER to EARLY AUTUMN
H 2m (6ft) S 2.5m (8ft)

From midsummer until early autumn, this dense evergreen shrub bears loose flowerheads of tiny, star-shaped flowers, their acid-yellow colour contrasting nicely with the bluish-green leaves. It is ideal for use in mild coastal gardens, where it can be grown as an informal hedge, but elsewhere it is best grown against a sheltered wall.

Callistemon citrinus 'Splendens'
Crimson bottlebrush
○ ❄ ⁂ pH→ –pH↓ ❖ SPRING, SUMMER
H 2m (6ft) S 1.5m (5ft)

Exotic-looking, crimson bottlebrush flower spikes, up to 15cm (6in) long, appear in spring and summer at the tips of lax, arching branches. The dark evergreen leaves release a lemon scent when rubbed. This shrub can be grown in mild coastal areas or inland against a sheltered, sunny wall. Elsewhere, try it in a large pot for the patio or conservatory.

Calluna vulgaris Heather, ling
○ ⬇⬇ pH↓ ❖SUMMER, AUTUMN, WINTER
H 20–60cm (8–24in) S 60–90cm
(2–3ft)

Calluna vulgaris varieties flower from midsummer to autumn in colours ranging from pure white to the darkest purple. All are evergreen; some have coloured or winter-tinted foliage, giving them year-round appeal. They make excellent ground-cover plants for open areas or over banks in sun on acid soil, but can also be used to edge sunny paths or provide structure to permanent displays in pots filled with ericaceous compost. Heather is loved by bees and other insects. Good varieties: 'Amethyst' (purplish-crimson flowers; H 30cm/12in, S 40cm/16in); 'Blazeaway' (lilac flowers, golden foliage becomes burnished in winter; H 35cm/14in, S 60cm/2ft); 'County Wicklow' (double, shell-pink flowers; H 25cm/10in, S 35cm/14in); 'Dark Beauty' (dark cerise flowers; H 25cm/10in, S 35cm/14in); 'Dark Star' (crimson flowers; H 20cm/8in, S 35cm/14in); 'H.E. Beale' (rose-pink flowers; H 60cm/2ft, S 90cm/3ft); 'Silver Knight' (mauve-pink flowers, silvery foliage with purple winter tints; H 40cm/16in, S 50cm/20in); 'Wickwar Flame' (mauve-pink flowers; H 50cm/20in, S 60cm/2ft).

Heathers and heaths

The native heather or ling (*Calluna vulgaris*) grows wild in Britain and its numerous cultivars are among the most reliable of flowering shrubs (*see* left). They need acid soil and flower from summer to autumn; many have colourful foliage and winter tints.

Heaths (*Erica* species, *see* pages 88–9) are similar to heathers and flower mainly in winter and spring (some are summer-flowering), but they have needle-like foliage rather than overlapping, scale-like leaves. The Cantabrian heath (*Daboecia cantabrica*, *see* page 86) flowers throughout summer and into autumn. Although heaths prefer acid soil and an open, sunny site, some varieties are more tolerant of lime than heathers and can tolerate partial shade.

Given the right soil conditions, heathers and heaths are easy to grow, provided they are not faced with too

Erica carnea 'Springwood White', an alpine heath, is low-spreading and bears white flowers from winter to early spring (*see also* page 88).

The purple-flowering heather *Calluna vulgaris* 'Spring Torch' makes a striking autumn display combined with the grass *Stipa tenuissima*.

much competition from other plants or weeds. Heathers do not like a rich soil and are best left unfed, because too many nutrients tend to make them become open and straggly.

All heathers and heaths are evergreen. To tidy, trim them with shears after flowering.

Camellia japonica
Common camellia

◐ ● ◖ pH↓ ❀ ❖MID-SPRING to LATE SPRING
H 9m (30ft) S 8m (26ft)

Spectacular single, red blooms appear in mid- to late-spring on a vigorous shrub with lustrous evergreen leaves. It is best in partial shade except in east-facing borders (early morning sun after frost can damage the flowers). Good varieties: 'Adolphe Audusson' (dark red flowers; H 5m/16ft, S 4m/13ft); 'Elegans' (dark rose-pink flowers; H and S 3m/10ft); 'Hagoromo' (semi-double, pale pink flowers; H 5m/16ft, S 4m/13ft); 'Nobilissima' (yellow-centred, white flowers from midwinter to early spring; H 5m/16ft, S 3m/10ft).

Camellia 'Leonard Messel'

◐ ● ◖ pH↓ ❀ ❖MID-SPRING
H 4m (13ft) S 3m (10ft)

This lovely evergreen shrub bears many semi-double, pink blooms in mid-spring. It is really hardy, ideal for colder gardens on acid soil. Ideally, grow it in a lightly shaded border where it is not exposed to early-morning sun. It can also be grown in tubs of ericaceous compost.

Camellia sasanqua 'Narumigata'
◐ ◑ ● ◖ pH↓ ❀ ❖LATE AUTUMN to WINTER
H 6m (20ft) S 3m (10ft)

This large, upright, evergreen shrub is smothered in scented, single, pink-tinted white flowers against glossy, dark green foliage. Unlike other camellias, it starts flowering in late autumn and continues into winter, when the rest of the garden can lack colour. It makes an interesting container plant (in ericaceous compost) and can be moved into a conservatory or cool greenhouse to flower.

Camellia × williamsii
◐ ● ◖ pH↓ ❀ ❖MID- to LATE SPRING
H 5m (16ft) S 3m (10ft)

Showy white to dark pink flowers bloom in mid- to late spring on an evergreen shrub with rounded leaves. Grow in acid soil, but not where morning sun after frost will damage the blooms. Good varieties: 'Anticipation' (crimson flowers; H 4m/13ft, S 2m/6ft); 'Debbie' (rose-pink flowers; H 3m/10ft, S 2m/6ft); 'Donation' (semi-double, soft-pink flowers; H 5m/16ft, S 2.5m/8ft); 'J.C. Williams' (single, pale pink flowers; H and S 5m/16ft).

Caragana arborescens Pea tree
○ ◔ ↓↓ ❖LATE SPRING
H 6m (20ft) S 4m (13ft)

An unusual upright, thorny shrub, this has very attractive pale green foliage and small clusters of bright yellow, pea-like flowers during late spring. Being tolerant of wind and dry soil, it is a good choice in exposed gardens where the soil is poor. Good variety: 'Nana' (smaller, with densely packed, distorted shoots; H 1.5m/5ft, S 4m/13ft; shown above).

Carpenteria californica 'Ladhams' Variety' Tree anemone
○ ❄ ↓↓ ❖EARLY to MIDSUMMER
H and S 2m (6ft)

When trained against a sheltered wall or fence, this stylish evergreen shrub can make an eye-catching display in early to midsummer. The large, fragrant, cup-shaped white flowers, up to 8cm (3in) across with a golden boss of stamens, shine out against a backdrop of glossy, dark green leaves. On well-established specimens, peeling brown bark is an attractive feature. It must have protection from cold winds.

Caryopteris × *clandonensis* 'Heavenly Blue' Bluebeard
○ ❄ ↓↓ ❖LATE SUMMER
H and S 1m (40in)

In late summer sprays of piercing dark blue flowers stand proud of the attractive mounds of toothed, aromatic, grey-green foliage. In really cold areas it is best planted in the shelter of tougher shrubs or against a sheltered wall or fence. Other good varieties: 'Kew Blue' (dark blue flowers); 'Worcester Gold' (lavender-blue flowers, golden foliage).

Ceanothus 'Autumnal Blue' California lilac
○ ❄ ↓↓ ❖LATE SUMMER to AUTUMN
H and S 3m (10ft)

Countless fluffy clusters of intensely blue flowers turn the whole shrub vivid blue from late summer into autumn. This upright evergreen is fully hardy, but it is best not to expose it to winter winds. Other good autumn-flowering varieties: 'Burkwoodii' (bright blue flowers; H 1.5m/5ft, S 2m/6ft); 'Perle Rose' (carmine-pink flowers; H and S 1.5m/5ft).

Ceanothus × *delileanus* 'Gloire de Versailles' California lilac
○ ❄ ↓↓ ❖LATE SUMMER
H 1.5m (5ft) S 2m (6ft)

This deservedly popular California lilac forms a compact, bushy shrub that is smothered in powder-blue flower clusters during late summer. Although fully hardy, it does best at the edge of a south- or west-facing border or against a sunny, sheltered wall.

Ceanothus arboreus 'Trewithen Blue' California lilac
○ ❄ ↓↓ ❖SPRING to EARLY SUMMER
H 6m (20ft) S 8m (26ft)

Having an open habit, this large ceanothus with fragrant mid-blue flowers does not catch the eye in the same way as more compact forms, but the individual flower clusters are much larger (up to 12cm/5in long). Although fully hardy, this upright evergreen does best at the back of a south- or west-facing bed or against a sunny, sheltered wall for protection from winter winds.

Ceanothus 'Blue Mound' California lilac
○ ❄ ↓↓ ❖EARLY SUMMER
H 1.5m (5ft) S 2m (6ft)

A lovely, compact, evergreen ceanothus, this is ideal for a sunny spot at the base of a sheltered wall or fence. In early summer the bold clusters of deep-blue flowers complement the dark, glossy, saw-edged foliage. Other good varieties: 'Concha' (reddish-purple buds opening to dark blue flowers; H and S 3m/10ft); 'Italian Skies' (bright blue flowers; H 1.5m/5ft, S 3m/10ft); 'Puget Blue' (dark blue flowers; H and S 3m/10ft).

Ceanothus thyrsiflorus Blueblossom
○ ❄ ↓↓ ❖LATE SPRING to EARLY SUMMER
H 2m (6ft) S 1.5m (5ft)

This ceanothus bears pale to deep-blue flowers set off by lustrous evergreen foliage. Protect from northerly winds by planting in a south- or west-facing border or against a sunny, sheltered wall. Good varieties: 'Millerton Point' (fragrant cream flowers; H and S 6m/20ft); var. *repens* (H 1m/40in, S 2.5m/8ft; low-spreading, fluffy, mid-blue flowers; shown above); 'Skylark' (dark blue flowers; H 2m/6ft, S 1.5m/5ft).

Ceratostigma griffithii
Hardy plumbago
○ ❄ 💧 ‡‡ ❖ LATE SUMMER to AUTUMN
H 1m (40in) S 1.5m (5ft)

A useful, domed, evergreen shrub that carries clusters of delightful bright blue flowers from late summer and into autumn, the hardy plumbago is ideal for softening the edges of a sunny path where the soil is well drained but does not dry out completely. Despite its common name, it is actually only frost hardy.

Ceratostigma willmottianum
'Forest Blue' Chinese plumbago
○ 💧 ‡‡ ❖ LATE SUMMER to AUTUMN
H 1m (40in) S 1.5m (5ft)

One of the best blue-flowered plants for the late-summer garden, this spreading shrub is clothed in purple-edged, dark green leaves that take on fiery autumn shades. The disc-like, brilliant blue flowers are produced from late summer and into autumn. It is ideal at the front of a sunny, sheltered border where the soil does not dry out in summer. Another good variety: 'Desert Skies' (golden foliage).

Chaenomeles speciosa
Flowering quince
○ ◐ 💧 ‡‡ ❖ SPRING to EARLY SUMMER, AUTUMN
H 2.5m (8ft) S 5m (16ft)

This vigorous shrub carries scarlet spring flowers that last until early summer on spiny branches. Aromatic, yellow-green fruits follow in autumn. It is useful for adding colour to east- and west-facing walls (prune it to form an upright shape). Good varieties: 'Geisha Girl' (apricot flowers, shown above; H 2m/6ft, S 1.2m/4ft); 'Moerloosei' (pale pink flowers); 'Nivalis' (white flowers).

Chaenomeles × superba
'Crimson and Gold'
Flowering quince
○ ◐ 💧 ‡‡ ❖ SPRING to EARLY SUMMER, AUTUMN
H 1m (40in) S 2m (6ft)

Loved for its startling deep-red flowers with golden stamens, this is a reliable, compact quince that can be trained on a wall, as a spiny hedge, or grown in a border. The flowers are followed by green fruits that ripen to yellow. Other good varieties: 'Jet Trail' (white flowers; H 60cm/2ft, S 2m/6ft); 'Pink Lady' (dark pink flowers; H 1.5m/5ft, S 2m/6ft).

Chimonanthus praecox
Wintersweet
○ ‡‡ ❖ WINTER to SPRING
H 4m (13ft) S 3m (10ft)

Heads turn when in deep winter this shrub produces its deliciously fragrant, sulphur-yellow flowers with purple centres on bare stems. They often last until mid-spring. Bring cut stems indoors. Place wintersweet in a sunny, sheltered spot near an entrance or a path so you can enjoy the scent. Good varieties: 'Grandiflorus' (darker yellow, less fragrant flowers); 'Luteus' (brighter flowers).

Choisya × dewitteana
'Aztec Pearl'
Mexican orange blossom
○ ◐ ❄ ‡‡ ❖ LATE SPRING, EARLY AUTUMN
H and S 2.5m (8ft)

This is a lovely variety with fabulously scented, star-shaped, pink-tinged white flowers in late spring and a later flush in early autumn. A compact, easy-to-grow evergreen with neat, aromatic, dark green foliage, it is ideal for a border in full sun or light shade, but needs shelter from severe weather. Choisya ternata 'Sundance' has yellow juvenile foliage.

Cistus × argenteus
'Peggy Sammons' Sun rose
○ ❄ ◊ ⬇⬇ ❖SUMMER
H and S 1m (40in)

This is a great little evergreen that bears a succession of pinkish-purple flowers over a mound of attractive, downy-grey leaves. It is an ideal candidate for the front of a sunny border, provided the soil is well drained and the shrub is not exposed to the coldest winter weather.

Cistus × lenis 'Grayswood Pink'
Sun rose
○ ❄ ◊ ⬇⬇ ❖SUMMER
H 75cm (30in) S 90cm (3ft)

This is a lovely, compact, hummock-forming, evergreen shrub that bears a succession of large, papery, silver-pink flowers (up to 8cm/3in across), which gradually bleach at the centre to almost white. The boss of golden stamens is the finishing touch. It is perfect for the front of a sunny border or a pot on the patio.

Cistus × purpureus 'Alan Fradd'
Sun rose
○ ❄ ◊ ⬇⬇ ❖SUMMER
H and S 1m (40in)

Large, white, tissue-paper flowers with a boss of golden stamens and daubed with maroon blobs at the base of the petals are produced on this attractive, rounded evergreen shrub. Red-tinted new shoots are a feature too. It is a good choice for the front of a sunny border.

Cistus × hybridus Sun rose
○ ❄ ◊ ⬇⬇ ❖SUMMER
H 1m (40in) S 1.5m (5ft)

A succession of glorious, golden-centred, papery, snow-white flowers open from crimson buds from early summer. Compact and easy to grow, this cistus will grace the front of a sunny border as long as it is not exposed to the coldest winter weather and the soil is well drained. Being evergreen, it makes an interesting year-round container plant.

Cistus × pulverulentus 'Sunset'
Sun rose
○ ❄ ◊ ⬇⬇ ❖SUMMER
H 60cm (2ft) S 90cm (3ft)

This pretty, evergreen shrub forms a neat mound of wavy-edged leaves covered in a profusion of rose-pink flowers, each with a golden eye of stamens. It is an ideal choice for alongside a patio or for covering a sheltered, sunny, well-drained bank.

Clerodendrum bungei
Glory flower
○ ❄ ● ⬇⬇ 🍃 ❖LATE SUMMER
H and S 2m (6ft)

This is an endearing, suckering shrub that bears large, dense, mophead-like clusters of fragrant, deep-pink flowers. However, it can be annoyingly invasive! Although it is less than hardy, if the roots are protected over winter it will resprout from below ground the following year.

Clethra alnifolia 'Paniculata'
Sweet pepper bush
◑ ◐ pH↓ 🍂 ❖LATE SUMMER
H and S 2.5m (8ft)

Spikes of scented white flowers appear from late summer on a deciduous shrub that is perfect for a shady border or a wildlife or woodland garden. The leaves turn butter yellow in autumn. Strongly upright, it can sucker and become invasive. Other good varieties: 'Pink Spire' (pink flower spikes); 'Rosea' (dark pink flower spikes).

Convolvulus cneorum
○ ❄ ↓↓ ❖EARLY SUMMER
H 60cm (2ft) S 90cm (3ft)

This lovely, compact, evergreen shrub carries white trumpets that open from twisted pink buds. The silver foliage has a metallic sheen in spring and early summer – a perfect foil for the flowers. It is an ideal candidate for growing in a patio pot or next to a sunny path.

Corokia cotoneaster
Wire-netting bush
○ ❄ ↓↓ ❖LATE SPRING
H and S 2.5m (8ft)

The bizarre, tangled mass of branches sparsely covered with tiny leaves has given rise to this evergreen shrub's apt common name. In late spring the curious tracery of stems is smothered in small, fragrant, bright yellow flowers, followed by orange fruits. It is a real talking point, but can be tricky to grow unless given full sun and shelter from cold, dry winds.

Coronilla valentina subsp. glauca 'Citrina'
○ ❄ – ❄ ↓↓ ❖LATE WINTER to MID-SPRING
H and S 80cm (32in)

A dense, bushy, evergreen shrub with blue-green foliage, this bears attractive fragrant, lemon-yellow, pea-like flowers from late winter until mid-spring. It is only borderline-hardy, so give it the protection of a warm, sunny wall or fence to guarantee winter survival.

Corylopsis pauciflora
○ ❄ ↓↓ pH↓ ❖EARLY SPRING
H 1.5m (5ft) S 2.5m (8ft)

This spreading, bushy shrub is well worth considering for a sheltered shrub border or a woodland garden, where it will provide early spring colour with its slightly fragrant, primrose-yellow, pendent flowers. The fresh green leaves have pretty pink tints as they emerge.

Cotoneaster franchetii
○ ◑ ↓↓ ❖EARLY SUMMER, AUTUMN
H and S 2m (6ft)

Cotoneasters have great value, doing well in difficult sites and bearing prolific, tiny white flowers followed by bright red berries loved by wildlife. This one is semi-evergreen, with arching branches and small, grey-green leaves. *C. horizontalis* is a deciduous species with herringbone-like branches; often grown on walls or banks (H 1m/40in, S 1.5m/5ft).

Cytisus 'Burkwoodii' Broom
○ ‖ pH→ –pH↓ ❖LATE SPRING to EARLY SUMMER
H and S 1.5m (5ft)

An adorable, compact shrub that bears lovely, yellow-edged, crimson flowers from late spring to early summer. It is an ideal choice where space is at a premium, especially if you cut back the tips of new growth after flowering to encourage bushiness. Other good varieties: 'Hollandia' (cream and pink flowers); 'Killiney Salmon' (salmon-pink and orange flowers; H 1.2m/4ft, S 1.5m/5ft); 'Lena' (deep-yellow flowers; H 1.2m/4ft, S 1.5m/5ft); 'Windlesham Ruby' (red flowers).

Cytisus × kewensis Broom
○ ‖ pH→ –pH↓ ❖EARLY SUMMER
H 30cm (12in) S 1.5m (5ft)

This charming, ground-hugging, prostrate broom is encrusted with characteristic pea-like flowers in a delicate shade of cream. It is a great choice for very poor soil, provided it is well drained. Prune after flowering to get the best display of flowers.

Cytisus × praecox 'Allgold' Broom
○ ‖ pH→ –pH↓ ❖MID-SPRING to EARLY SUMMER
H 1.2m (4ft) S 1.5m (5ft)

This floriferous, compact broom produces long-lasting, bright yellow, pea-like flowers from mid-spring on elegant arching stems. It is one of the earliest brooms to flower and is the perfect choice for a sunny spot with well-drained soil. Other good varieties: 'Albus' (white flowers); 'Warminster' (creamy-yellow flowers).

Cytisus scoparius 'Cornish Cream' Broom
○ ‖ pH→ –pH↓ ❖LATE SPRING to EARLY SUMMER
H and S 1.5m (5ft)

An abundance of charming white and creamy-yellow, pea-like flowers are produced on delicate, wand-like shoots above this compact and bushy shrub. It is an ideal choice for a sunny spot in any sized garden, particularly growing alongside a path or patio.

Daboecia cantabrica subsp. scotica 'Silverwells'
Cantabrian heath
○ ‖ pH→ –pH↓ ❖SUMMER to AUTUMN
H 45cm (18in) S 75cm (30in)

This is a late summer flowering heath that blooms for ages. Dapper, urn-shaped, white flowers are held on slim, upright spikes above mounds of dark, evergreen foliage. It is an ideal ground-cover plant on acid soil, looking fantastic when grown in bold drifts, and makes a good container plant, too. *See also* Heathers and heaths, page 80.

Daphne bholua
○ ◐ ◌ ‖ ❧ ❖LATE WINTER
H 4m (13ft) S 1.5m (5ft)

This enchanting, upright, evergreen shrub bears clusters of sweetly fragrant, pinkish-mauve, late-winter flowers that stand out against lance-shaped, dark green leaves. Fleshy black berries follow. It is ideal for a mixed or shrub border in light shade, or next to a well-used shady path or entrance, so you can appreciate the delightful fragrance. Good varieties: 'Darjeeling' (H 3m/10ft, S 1.5m/5ft); 'Jacqueline Postill' (purple-pink flowers).

Daphne × burkwoodii 'Somerset'

○ ◑ ❄ ◐ ‡‡ 🍂 ❖LATE SPRING
H 1.5m (5ft) S 1m (40in)

This daphne is a useful, semi-evergreen shrub for a garden where space is at a premium. It bears delightful clusters of fragrant, pink blooms with paler lobes on short, stubby side branches during late spring and, in a good year, may also bloom again In autumn.

Daphne mezereum Mezereon

○ ◑ ◐ ‡‡ 🍂 ❖LATE WINTER to SPRING, SUMMER
H 1.2m (4ft) S 1m (40in)

The best feature of this super little shrub is the eye-catching clusters of highly fragrant, purplish-pink flowers on bare stems in late winter and early spring. They are followed by red fruits. It also has attractive grey-green leaves. It is a good choice for winter interest in a cottage-style border.

Daphne odora 'Aureomarginata'

○ ◑ ❄ ◐ ‡‡ 🍂 ❖WINTER, SPRING
H and S 1.5m (5ft)

This is a highly fragrant, rounded, evergreen shrub with handsome yellow-edged leaves that fade to white with age. Clusters of sweetly scented, reddish-purple winter flowers are followed by fleshy red berries. It is hardy, but only just. It is ideal either in a mixed or shrub border in light shade, or next to a door or a well-used shady path so the fragrance can be fully enjoyed.

Desfontainia spinosa

◑ ❄ ◐ ‡‡ pH→ –pH↓ ❖SUMMER to LATE AUTUMN
H and S 2m (6ft)

A beautiful, dense, bushy evergreen shrub with prickly, holly-like leaves, this is decorated with bright red, tubular flowers tipped in glowing gold from midsummer and through the autumn. It can cope with partial shade but needs shelter from cold winds.

Deutzia × hybrida 'Mont Rose'

○ ◑ ‡‡ pH→ –pH↓ ❖MIDSUMMER
H and S 1.2m (4ft)

Small, dainty, rose-pink, midsummer flowers that bring apple blossom to mind are produced in clusters on arching stems clothed in rounded leaves. Very free-flowering, this compact shrub blooms best in full sun, but will grow in partial shade. It is a good choice for small gardens.

Diervilla × splendens

Bush honeysuckle

○ ◑ ‡‡ ❖SUMMER
H 1.2m (4ft) S 1.5m (5ft)

This is an attractive and unusual filler shrub that looks a bit like weigela, but with clusters of sulphur-yellow flowers held above the puckered, purple-tinged green leaves in summer. It is a suckering shrub, and spreads.

Dipelta floribunda
○ ◑ ↕ pH→–pH↓ ❖LATE SPRING to EARLY SUMMER
H and S 4m (13ft)

This is an unusual shrub that deserves wider use. It forms an attractive, upright, multi-stemmed specimen clothed in pointed pale foliage. In late spring and early summer it produces clusters of tubular, pale pink flowers with canary-yellow throats. It is hard to propagate, so difficult to find.

Erica arborea var. alpina
'Albert's Gold' Tree heath
○ ↕ pH→–pH↓ ❖SPRING
H 2m (6ft) S 80cm (32in)

This tree heath is an underrated shrub. A large, upright evergreen, it has glowing golden, needle-like foliage and clusters of honey-scented, greyish-white flowers in spring. It needs a sunny site and well-drained soil. Recommended for neutral to acid soil, it also tolerates lime.

Erica carnea Alpine heath
○ ◑ ↕ pH↓ ❖LATE WINTER, EARLY SPRING
H 15cm (6in) S 45cm (18in)

There are numerous varieties of this popular winter-flowering heather, ranging in colour from white to pink and deep purple-red. The low-spreading, evergreen bushes are smothered in flowers in late winter or early spring, ideal for an alpine or gravel bed, or for adding colour to a winter container planting. They tolerate moderately chalky soil and some shade. Good pink varieties: 'Ann Sparkes' (rose-pink flowers darken with age, burnished gold foliage, bronze-tipped in spring; H 25cm/10in, S 45cm/18in); 'Challenger' (magenta flowers); 'December Red' (pink flowers darken to purplish red); 'Foxhollow' (purplish-pink flowers, bronze-tipped yellow foliage; H 15cm/6in, S 40cm/16in); 'King George' (deep-pink flowers; H 15cm/6in, S 25cm/10in); 'Myretoun Ruby' (rose-pink flowers age to crimson-red; shown above); 'Pink Spangles' (shell-pink flowers); 'Rosalie' (bright pink flowers, bronze-green leaves); 'Vivellii' (bronze winter foliage, pink flowers become magenta with age; H and S 35cm/14in). Good white-flowered varieties: 'Golden Starlet' (lime-yellow foliage); 'Springwood White' (bright green foliage); 'Whitehall' (H 15cm/ 6in, S 30cm/12in).
See also Heathers and heaths, page 80.

Erica × darleyensis 'J.W. Porter'
Darley Dale heath
○ ↕ ❖LATE WINTER, SPRING
H 25cm (10in) S 40cm (16in)

This useful heath can grow in any well-drained soil. Plant it in bold drifts to create a sea of winter colour when the purplish-pink, urn-shaped flowers appear. The dark green foliage has attractive cream and red tints in spring. Other good varieties: 'Darley Dale' (shell-pink flowers, cream-tipped leaves in spring; H 15cm/6in, S 55cm/22in); 'Furzey' (lilac-pink flowers and pink-tipped leaves in spring; H 35cm/14in, S 60cm/2ft).

Erica tetralix 'Pink Star'
Cross-leaved heath
○ ◗ ↕ pH↓ ❖MIDSUMMER to MID-AUTUMN
H 20cm (8in) S 30cm (12in)

A low-spreading, grey-leaved evergreen shrub, the cross-leaved heath bears clusters or whorls of lilac-pink flowers from midsummer to mid-autumn. Plant it in bold drifts in acid soil. Other good varieties: 'Alba Mollis' (white flowers); 'Con Underwood' (magenta flowers).

Erica vagans 'Lyonesse'
Cornish heather
○ ⇊ pH→ –pH↓ ❖SUMMER to AUTUMN
H 25cm (10in) S 50cm (20in)

Long-lasting, white, bell-shaped flowers are produced from summer to autumn when this heather is planted in an open site. Like all heathers, it is evergreen. Being lime-tolerant, it can be used in new gardens with well-drained soil that is rich in builders' rubble. Another good variety: 'Mrs D.F. Maxwell' (deep-pink flowers; H 30cm/12in, S 45cm/18in).

Escallonia 'Apple Blossom'
○ ❄ ⇊ ❖SUMMER
H and S 2.5m (8ft)

Masses of pretty, pale pink flowers like apple blossom appear throughout summer, resplendent against the glossy, dark green foliage of this bushy evergreen shrub. It forms a lovely informal, flowering hedge in a sheltered spot. Other good varieties: 'Iveyi' (white flowers; H and S 3m/10ft); 'Peach Blossom' (peach and white flowers H 2.5m/8ft); 'Red Elf' (dark crimson flowers; H 2m/6ft, S 4m/13ft).

Exochorda × *macrantha* 'The Bride' Pearl bush
○ ◐ ❄ 💧 ⇊ ❖LATE SPRING
H and S 2m (6ft)

Wall-to-wall flowers are what you get with this floriferous shrub. Pretty, white, late-spring blooms smother elegant weeping branches for a month or more. It flowers best in full sun but is also good at the front of a border in partial shade where it gets some direct sun.

Fabiana imbricata
○ ❄ ⇊ pH→ –pH↓ ❖EARLY SUMMER
H and S 2.5m (8ft)

An unusual-looking, mound-forming evergreen shrub that looks a bit like a tree heath with plume-like branches covered in needle-like leaves. The branches carry tubular, mauve to white flowers during early summer. Plant it in a sheltered spot where it is protected from cold winds. Good variety: 'Prostrata' (white flowers, hardier than the species; H 1m/40in, S 2m/6ft).

Fatsia japonica Japanese aralia
○ ◐ ● ❄ 💧 ⇊ ❖AUTUMN
H and S 4m (13ft)

This is an architectural giant grown for its huge, fig-shaped, glossy evergreen leaves, which help reflect light into dark corners. In autumn, large lollipop-clusters of creamy flowers are a bonus, followed by rounded, black fruits. It looks tough, but is not actually fully hardy. It makes an excellent focal point for a border, sheltered from cold winds.

Forsythia × *intermedia* 'Lynwood Variety'
○ ◐ 💧 ⇊ ❖SPRING
H and S 3m (10ft)

This brings early-spring 'sunshine' to a shady plot when its bare branches are thick with bright yellow flowers. At other times fairly uninteresting to look at, it is ideal for placing at the back of a border where it can remain unnoticed, or act as a foil for other flowering plants. It also makes an attractive, informal hedge. Other good varieties: 'Beatrix Farrand'; 'Spectabilis'; 'Spectabilis Variegated' (cream-variegated leaves).

Fothergilla major
○ ◐ ◦ ⇅ pH↓ ❖EARLY SUMMER, AUTUMN
H 2.5m (8ft) S 2m (6ft)

This is grown for its fiery autumnal show, when its lustrous, dark green foliage turns shades of red, orange and yellow. White, bottlebrush-like, scented flowers are an early-summer bonus. It colours-up best in full sun, but is lovely as an understorey plant in a woodland garden, or in dappled shade where it catches the morning or evening sun in autumn.

Fremontodendron
'California Glory' Flannel bush
○ ❀ pH↔–pH↓ ❖LATE SPRING to AUTUMN
H 6m (20ft) S 4m (13ft)

Waxy-looking, canary-yellow, saucer-shaped flowers borne from late spring to autumn are the main feature of this magnificent, not-so-hardy, woody, climbing shrub. The leathery, lobed, dark evergreen leaves are attractive at other times. Plant it in a sunny, sheltered spot where it is protected from cold winds.

Fuchsia 'Riccartonii'
○ ◐ ❀ ◦ ⇅ ❖SUMMER to AUTUMN
H 2m (6ft) S 3m (10ft)

This tall fuchsia sports scarlet and dark purple flowers, from midsummer to autumn, and bronze-tinted foliage. One of the hardiest 'hardy' fuchsias (hardy, but only just), it is a good front-of-border shrub if protected from cold winds. It makes a fine informal hedge, too. Other good varieties: 'Mrs Popple' (scarlet and violet flowers; H and S 1m/40in); 'Snowcap' (red and white flowers; H and S 50cm/20in); 'Tom Thumb' (red and mauve flowers; H and S 30cm/12in).

Garrya elliptica 'James Roof'
Silk-tassel bush
○ ◐ ⇅ ❖WINTER
H and S 4m (13ft)

This utilitarian, pollution-tolerant shrub, often seen covering urban walls and fences with a cloak of wavy-edged, evergreen foliage, is lit up in winter by elegant, silvery male catkins up to 20cm (8in) long. It is a good foil for other plants during the growing season.

Gaultheria procumbens
Wintergreen
◐ ◦ pH↓ 🍂 ❖EARLY SUMMER, AUTUMN
H 15cm (6in) S 1m (40in)

In early summer, lily-of-the-valley-like, white or pale pink flowers, followed by aromatic scarlet fruits in autumn, are set off against glossy dark, evergreen foliage. In winter the leaves tinge red. This creeping shrub is ideal for carpeting the ground between larger shrubs and trees, or for providing a permanent edge to acid woodland paths, where the foliage, when lightly crushed underfoot, will perfume the air with the heady aroma of wintergreen.

Genista hispanica Spanish gorse
○ ❀ ⇅ ❖LATE SPRING to SUMMER
H 75cm (30in) S 1.5m (5ft)

Golden showers of flowers reliably decorate spiny, pale green stems on this dense, spreading shrub. Bear in mind that it is not so hardy, so it should be planted in a sheltered spot. Prune back the tips of this gorse after flowering to maintain a bushy habit.

Genista lydia Broom
○ ↓↓ ❖EARLY SUMMER
H 60cm (2ft) S 1m (40in)

Canary-yellow flowers are produced *en masse* during early summer, covering the spreading, greyish-green branches, which arch at the tips. This is a really magnificent, if prickly, compact broom and it looks great in a gravel garden.

× *Halimiocistus* 'Ingwersenii'
○ ❄ – ❄ ↓↓ ❖LATE SPRING to LATE SUMMER
H 45cm (18in) S 90cm (3ft)

If you have a sunny spot you might like to try this low-growing evergreen. It is covered in pretty white flowers, like rock roses, all summer. Happiest in well-drained, poor to moderately fertile soil, it is ideal at the front of a sunny border, or at the base of a sunny wall, sheltered from cold winds. In fertile soil or in shade, it is only borderline-hardy, but since it is easy to propagate you can insure against winter losses.

Hamamelis × *intermedia*
Witch hazel
○ ◑ ◔ pH↓ 🌿 ❖AUTUMN, WINTER
H and S 4m (13ft)

Distinctive, sweetly scented, spidery winter flowers are borne on bare stems. Attractive pale green foliage helps lift the gloom in summer, and in autumn takes on butter-yellow and burnished-orange tints. The curiously eye-catching flowers stand out against the dark evergreen foliage of other acid-loving understorey shrubs in dappled areas. Good varieties: 'Arnold Promise' (yellow flowers); 'Diane' (red flowers); 'Jelena' (coppery-red flowers); 'Pallida' (sulphur-yellow flowers; H and S 3m/10ft).

Hebe albicans
○ ◑ ❄ ↓↓ pH→ – pH↑ ❖EARLY SUMMER
H 60cm (2ft) S 90cm (3ft)

This compact hebe, with greyish-green leaves that are retained throughout the year, becomes smothered in densely packed, white flower spikes during early summer. Being pollution- and salt-tolerant, it is ideal if you are in a mild urban area or on the coast.

Hebe 'Great Orme'
○ ◑ ❄ ↓↓ pH→ – pH↑ ❖ SUMMER
H and S 1.2m (4ft)

Offering great garden value, this evergreen, long-flowering shrub will light up any spot in full sun or dappled shade. From midsummer its elegant spikes of bright pink flowers fade to white. Plant it in a sheltered area where cold winds cannot damage it. Other good varieties: 'Midsummer Beauty' (lavender flowers; H 2m/6ft, S 1.5m/5ft); 'Pewter Dome' (white flowers; H 40cm/16in, S 60cm/2ft).

Hebe pinguifolia 'Pagei'
○ ◑ ❄ ↓↓ pH→ – pH↑ ❖LATE SPRING to SUMMER
H 45cm (18in) S 60cm (2ft)

A practically prostrate evergreen, this superb hebe makes excellent ground cover for the edge of a sunny border. Its chunky, blue-green foliage looks good all year, but especially when snow-white flowers are produced on purple stems *en masse* in late spring and early summer. It tolerates salt and pollution, so is a good choice for mild coastal or urban gardens.

Hebe rakaiensis Shrubby veronica
○ ◐ ◌ ‖ pH→–pH↑ ❖EARLY SUMMER
H 1m (40in) S 1.2m (4ft)

A utilitarian, rounded, evergreen shrub, this hebe is really tough and resilient. Frothy spikes of large, white flowers in early summer stand proud of neat mounds of glossy, fresh green leaves. It is ideal for making a low hedge and for adding substance to mixed borders, and it is useful in oriental-style gardens too.

Hebe 'Red Edge'
○ ◐ ❄ ‖ pH→–pH↑ ❖SUMMER
H 45cm (18in) S 60cm (2ft)

Although its dainty, lilac-blue flowers, which fade to white during the summer, are adorable, it is usually for the densely packed, red-edged, greyish-green leaves that this is grown. It makes an excellent low or informal, evergreen hedge. Plant it in a sheltered spot where it is protected from cold winter winds.

Helianthemum 'Ben Fhada'
Rock rose
○ ‖ pH→–pH↑ ❖EARLY SUMMER
H and S 30cm (12in)

Rock roses are slightly unkempt, low-growing, evergreen shrubs. This one bears a succession of orange-centred, golden, saucer-shaped flowers in early summer. It looks great in a gravel garden or spilling over the edge of a path. Other good varieties: 'Amy Baring' (apricot flowers; H 10cm/4in, S 30cm/12in); 'Ben Heckla' (orange-centred, brick-red flowers); 'Chocolate Blotch' (chocolate-centred, pale orange flowers).

Hibiscus syriacus 'Oiseau Bleu'
Tree hollyhock
○ ‖ pH→–pH↑ ❖LATE SUMMER to AUTUMN
H 3m (10ft) S 2m (6ft)

Often labelled 'Blue Bird', this bears a succession of maroon-centred, violet-blue trumpets from late summer into autumn. It will add an exotic feel to a sheltered, sunny border. Other good varieties: 'Hamabo' (pinkish-white flowers; H 2m/6ft, S 1m/40in); 'Lavender Chiffon' (double, lavender flowers); 'Woodbridge' (deep-pink flowers).

Hydrangea arborescens 'Annabelle'
○ ◐ ◌ ‖ ✿ ❖LATE SUMMER
H and S 2.5m (8ft)

This is superb for dappled shade, where its balls of tightly packed, creamy flowers sing out in late summer. The flowerheads fade gracefully as they mature, and the two-tone leaves turn yellow. It is ideal at the back of a mixed border on moist soil.

Hydrangea macrophylla
Common hydrangea
○ ◐ ◌ ‖ ✿ ❖MID- to LATE SUMMER
H 2m (6ft) S 2.5m (8ft)

These familiar shrubs fall into two groups: mopheads, with rounded flowerheads; and lacecaps, which are lighter and flatter, with a boss of small florets ringed by larger florets. All flower in mid- to late summer (the heads can be dried) and are ideal in a border or tub. On acid soil, the flowers on some pink varieties are blue (see page 29). Good mopheads: 'Ayesha' (mauve-pink; H 1.5m/5ft, S 2m/6ft); 'Madame Emile Mouillère' (white with a blue eye). Good lacecaps: 'Mariesii Perfecta' (pink to deep blue; shown above); 'Veitchii' (white, aging to pink).

Hydrangea paniculata 'Grandiflora'

○ ◐ 💧 ‖ 🐛 ✿ LATE SUMMER to EARLY AUTUMN
H 3m (10ft) S 2.5m (8ft)

A real showstopper, this! In late summer and early autumn, huge cones of creamy-white flowers, aging gracefully to pink, burst forth from large mounds of dark green foliage. Other good varieties: 'Vanille Fraise' (new, compact variety with creamy-white flowers that age first to pink, then turn red; H 2m/6ft, S 1.5m/5ft).

Hydrangea 'Preziosa'

○ ◐ 💧 ‖ 🐛 ✿ LATE SUMMER
H and S 1.5m (5ft)

Ideal for a small garden, this compact hydrangea offers fabulous autumn colour. The young foliage is purple-tinged. Dainty clusters of flowers appear in late summer – on acid soil, these are red and blue, becoming deep red-purple. It is ideal towards the back of a mixed border with moist soil.

Hypericum 'Hidcote'
St John's wort

○ ◐ ❄ 💧 ‖ 🐛 ✿ MIDSUMMER to EARLY AUTUMN
H 1.2m (4ft) S 1.5m (5ft)

This versatile, long-flowering, evergreen shrub can be used in a mixed border or a shrub border in sun or dappled shade. It forms an impenetrable thicket that becomes the centre of attention when it is covered in uplifting, golden-yellow, saucer-shaped flowers from midsummer onwards. It is not as tough as it looks, however, so needs protecting from cold, drying winds.

Indigofera heterantha Indigo

○ ‖ ✿ SUMMER
H and S 3m (10ft)

Elegant, arching branches carry spikes of rose-purple, pea-like flowers throughout the summer months, set off by the rather sumptuous, feathery, grey-green foliage. It is late coming into leaf, so the delicate foliage on this spreading shrub looks fresh throughout the summer.

Itea ilicifolia

○ ❄ ‖ ✿ LATE SUMMER
H and S 3m (10ft)

This is a real talking point, and worth considering if you have the space. It is an understated, fountain-shaped evergreen shrub with dark green, holly-like foliage, but the highlight during late summer is the amazing crop of cascading tassels – 45cm (18in) long – of tiny, fragrant, greenish-white flowers. Plant it in a sheltered spot where it will be protected from cold winter winds.

Jasminum nudiflorum
Winter jasmine

○ ◐ ‖ 🐛 ✿ WINTER
H and S 3m (10ft)

Uplifting, sunny-yellow, tubular flowers appear on bare green, arching stems from midwinter on, brightening up dingy days when little else is in bloom. It is reliable and very easy to grow, and can be trained against a wall or fence or left to make an informal clump.

Kalmia angustifolia f. *rubra*
Sheep laurel
◐💧pH↓🌿 ❖EARLY SUMMER
H 60cm (2ft) S 1.5m (5ft)

Dark rosy-red, bowl-shaped, early-summer flowers are borne on this mounding evergreen shrub with dark green leaves. It can take a few years to settle in before flowering, but it is worth the wait. It is an ideal understorey plant for the dappled areas beneath deciduous trees as part of a woodland scheme.

Kalmia latifolia Calico bush
○◐💧pH↓🌿 ❖EARLY SUMMER
H and S 3m (10ft)

Rhododendron-like, bowl-shaped, pale pink or white, early-summer flowers open from dark pink buds and seem to glow against a backdrop of glossy, dark evergreen foliage. It makes an interesting addition to an acid shrub border in sun or partial shade. Good variety: 'Ostbo Red' (red flowers).

Kerria japonica Japanese rose
○◐❄ ‖ ❖EARLY SPRING
H 2m (6ft) S 2.5m (8ft)

Uplifting, golden, buttercup-like, early flowers are produced on stiffly arching stems with attractive emerging fresh green foliage. This is an easy-to-grow utilitarian shrub that will succeed almost anywhere, but bear in mind it can throw up suckers. Good varieties: 'Golden Guinea' (large flowers); 'Picta' (orange-yellow flowers, white-variegated leaves; H 1.5m/5ft, S 2m/6ft); 'Pleniflora' (double flowers; H and S 3m/10ft).

Kolkwitzia amabilis
'Pink Cloud' Beauty bush
○◐ ‖ ❖EARLY SUMMER
H 3m (10ft) S 4m (13ft)

This is a quick-growing filler shrub that looks stunning during early summer when smothered in pale to deep-pink, bell-shaped flowers that hang elegantly from arching branches. A tolerant and easy-to-grow plant, it is a great choice for a beginner gardener.

Lavandula angustifolia
'Munstead' Lavender
○💧‖ ❖SUMMER
H 45cm (18in) S 60cm (2ft)

One of the best purple lavenders, this has dense spikes of flowers above a mound of aromatic, grey-green leaves. It makes an ideal fragrant evergreen edge to a path, and the flowers dry well for pot-pourri and sachets. Other good varieties: 'Hidcote' (deep-violet flowers; H 60cm/2ft, S 75cm/30in); 'Nana Alba' (white flowers; H and S 30cm/12in); 'Rosea' (rose-pink flowers; H and S 75cm/30in); 'Royal Purple' (purple-blue flowers; H and S 75cm/30in).

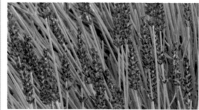

Lavandula × *intermedia* 'Grosso'
English lavender
○💧‖ ❖SUMMER
H 30cm (12in) S 40cm (16in)

This compact, evergreen, grey-leaved lavender is athrong with bees and other insects from midsummer, when the slender spikes of purple-violet flowers open. It is ideal for adding summer colour to a wildlife area. Another good variety: 'Pale Pretender' (bluish-purple flowers; H 1m/40in, S 1.5m/5ft).

Lavandula pedunculata subsp. *pedunculata* ('Papillon')
Butterfly lavender, French lavender
○ ❄ ◇ ‼ ❖SUMMER
H and S 60cm (24in)

This lavender is loved for the butterfly-like bracts that flutter on top of the stubby flower spikes appearing in summer and sometimes extending into autumn. It needs shelter from winter cold and wet, but, given that, it is a great choice for a sunny Mediterranean-style garden. In colder areas try it in a large tub, so you can give it protection.

Lavatera × *clementii* 'Barnsley' Mallow
○ ‼ ❖SUMMER
H and S 2m (6ft)

A fast-growing semi-evergreen, this fountain-shaped shrub bears a succession of white, hollyhock-like blooms, flushed pink at the centre, from midsummer. It has a tendency to 'revert' to an all-pink form unless affected stems are pruned out. Another good variety: 'Burgundy Wine' (veined, deep-pink flowers).

Leucothoe fontanesiana
Switch ivy
◑ ● ◌ pH↓ 🌿 ❖EARLY SPRING
H 2m (6ft) S 3m (10ft)

This is an upright, bushy evergreen with arching stems that carry clusters of white, urn-shaped, early-spring flowers. It is ideal for shade – even deep shade between buildings. It needs acid soil, but can be grown in a large pot in lime-free compost. Good varieties: 'Rainbow' (dappled cream and pink; H 1.5m/5ft, S 2m/6ft); *L.* 'Scarletta' (emerging leaves red-purple; H 1.5m/5ft, S 40cm/16in).

Leycesteria formosa
Himalayan honeysuckle
○ ◑ ❄ ❖LATE SUMMER, AUTUMN
H and S 2m (6ft)

This is grown for its long-lasting hanging clusters of white flowers and purple-red bracts in late summer. Purple berries follow, much loved by birds. It is hardy, but only just, and a good choice for a mixed border in sun or partial shade that is protected from severe winter weather.

Lonicera fragrantissima
○ ◑ ‼ ❖LATE WINTER to EARLY SPRING
H 2m (6ft) S 3m (10ft)

Highly fragrant, creamy-white flowers are borne during mild weather in late winter and early spring, and are followed by red berries. This lovely deciduous or semi-evergreen shrub is happy in a sun-blessed border or one in dappled shade. Plant it near an entrance or path so you can appreciate the fragrance, or train it on a wall or fence.

Lonicera × *purpusii* 'Winter Beauty' Winter honeysuckle
○ ◑ ‼ ❖WINTER
H 2m (6ft) S 2.5m (8ft)

A joy in the winter garden, when its fragrant clusters of white, tubular flowers with prominent yellow anthers decorate bare branches, this makes a rounded shrub with purple-stained shoots and dark green leaves. Choose it for a mixed border, or plant it next to a path and breathe in the lovely winter fragrance as you walk past.

Magnolia liliiflora 'Nigra'

○ ◑ pH→ –pH↓ 🌿 ❖EARLY SUMMER to AUTUMN

H 3m (10ft) S 2.5m (8ft)

Extend the enjoyment of magnolias from early summer into autumn with this beautiful variety with purple-red, goblet-shaped flowers. The blooms will be produced on and off into the autumn too. Being compact, it is a good choice where space is limited.

Magnolia stellata Star magnolia

○ ◑ 🌿 ❖SPRING

H 3m (10ft) S 4m (13ft)

Brilliant white, slightly scented, star-shaped flowers open from silky buds on bare branches in early spring. It makes a compact, bushy specimen that is ideal for small gardens and can survive in alkaline soils if moist. It can also be grown in half-barrel containers. Good varieties: 'Royal Star' (pink-flushed buds); 'Waterlily' (many-petalled flowers).

Mahonia aquifolium 'Apollo'
Oregon grape

◐ ● ❖SPRING

H 1m (40in) S 1.5m (5ft)

Ideal for shade, this mahonia bears impressive, lumpy clusters of fragrant, acid-yellow flowers in spring, above fresh green, holly-like, evergreen foliage, which takes on purple tints in winter. Another good variety: 'Smaragd' (more upright, new foliage bronzed, bright yellow flowers; H 60cm/2ft, S 1m/40in).

Mahonia japonica
Japanese barberry

◐ ● ❖WINTER

H 2m (6ft) S 3m (10ft)

This superb, architectural evergreen is characterized by its ruffs of dark green, holly-like leaves on upright woody stems topped by slender spikes of pale yellow winter flowers that have a lily-of-the-valley fragrance. It makes a useful understorey plant for a woodland edge or shrub border in shade. Good varieties: Bealei Group (shorter flower spikes).

Mahonia × *media* 'Charity'

◐ ● ❖WINTER

H 5m (16ft) S 4m (13ft)

Spiny evergreen foliage on upright woody stems makes this a good barrier against intruders. In winter, dark yellow flower spikes erupt from the whorls of leaves. Other good varieties: 'Buckland' (winter-foliage tints); 'Lionel Fortescue' (pale yellow flowers); 'Underway' (bright yellow flowers); 'Winter Sun' (fragrant, bright yellow, erect flower spikes).

Myrtus communis subsp. *tarentina* Myrtle

○ ❄ ❖LATE SUMMER

H and S 1.5m (5ft)

This super little evergreen myrtle can be grown in any sunny garden that provides shelter in winter. It could also be grown in a container and overwintered in a conservatory. Throughout late summer it produces scented, pink-flushed, cream-coloured flowers, followed by white berries. The glossy, dark green leaves are aromatic too.

Olearia × haastii Daisy bush
○ ❖LATE SUMMER
H 2m (6ft) S 3m (10ft)

During late summer this aptly named daisy bush is smothered with pretty, yellow-centred white blooms. Its small, evergreen leaves are felted silver beneath. This is one of the hardiest olearias and, being wind- and salt-tolerant, makes a good choice for coastal sites.

Osmanthus × burkwoodii
○ ◐ ‡‡ 🍂 ❖LATE SPRING
H and S 3m (10ft)

A deservedly popular evergreen shrub, this is prized for its beautiful, delightfully fragrant, jasmine-like, white flowers produced throughout late spring. Lustrous, finely toothed, dark green leaves give it a border presence at other times. It is a perfect structural addition to a shrub border or mixed border and a good choice for an Eastern-inspired garden design.

Osmanthus delavayi
○ ◐ ‡‡ 🍂 ❖LATE SPRING
H 6m (20ft) S 4m (13ft)

Arching branches bear marvellously fragrant, white, jasmine-like flowers throughout late spring on this domed evergreen. At other times, handsome, jagged-edged, lustrous, dark grey-green leaves are a fine foil for nearby flowers. Plant it in a border or beside a well-used path or entrance to appreciate the scent.

Osmanthus heterophyllus
○ ◐ ❋ ‡‡ 🍂 ❖LATE SUMMER, AUTUMN
H and S 5m (16ft)

Worth growing for its lustrous, holly-like leaves alone, this neat, dome-shaped evergreen also offers scented, tubular flowers in late summer, then blue-black berries. It is an ideal structural plant for a sheltered border in light shade. Good varieties: 'Aureomarginatus' (yellow-edged leaves); 'Goshiki' (leaves emerge creamy gold and bronze; hardier than species; H 1.5m/5ft, S 1m/40in); 'Gulftide' (very spiny leaves, H 2.5m/8ft, S 3m/10ft); 'Purpureus' (leaves emerge deep purple).

Paeonia ludlowii Peony
○ ◐ ❋ ◌ ‡‡ ❖LATE SPRING
H and S 2.5m (8ft)

This is a fantastic, free-flowering tree peony – it is difficult to find, but worth tracking down. It bears superb, slightly nodding, saucer-shaped, golden-yellow flowers, up to 12cm (5In) across, over a dense mound of lush foliage that emerges bronze-tinted in spring. It is an excellent choice for a border specimen and it looks great in containers too.

Paeonia suffruticosa Moutan
○ ◐ ◌ ‡‡ ❖LATE SPRING
H and S 2.2m (7ft)

Huge, cup-shaped, white, pink or red, late-spring flowers, up to 30cm (12in) across, are carried over a mound of attractive divided foliage that contrasts well with other shrubs. It is difficult to propagate, so difficult to find. Good varieties: 'Cardinal Vaughan' (semi-double, ruby-red flowers); 'Duchess of Kent' (semi-double, scarlet flowers); 'Mrs William Kelway' (double, white flowers).

Philadelphus coronarius
'Aureus' Mock orange
◑ ↕↕ ❖EARLY SUMMER
H 2.5m (8ft) S 1.5m (5ft)

Although this lovely, golden mock orange is grown mainly for its colourful foliage, the saucer-shaped, cream-coloured flowers with orange-blossom fragrance are a delight during early summer too. Use it to light up the back of a mixed border or to provide foliage contrast in a shrub border in dappled shade.

Philadelphus 'Manteau
d'Hermine' Mock orange
○ ◑ ↕↕ ❖EARLY to MIDSUMMER
H 75cm (30in) S 1.5m (5ft)

Ideal for small gardens, this compact mock orange bears masses of headily fragrant, cup-shaped, creamy flowers. Plant it in a sheltered spot, ideally next to a seating area, to enjoy its scent to the full. Other good varieties: 'Belle Etoile' (single, maroon-flushed, white flowers from late spring to summer; H 1.2m/4ft, S 2.5m/8ft); 'Virginal' (double, white flowers; H 3m/10ft, S 2.5m/8ft).

Phlomis fruticosa
Jerusalem sage
○ ❄ ↕↕ ❖EARLY SUMMER
H 1m (40in) S 1.5m (5ft)

This is a useful evergreen shrub with aromatic, lance-shaped, grey-green, sage-like foliage and striking whorls of hooded, butter-yellow flowers in early summer. It is a good choice for a sunny bank, gravel garden or Mediterranean-style planting, but needs protection from cold winds and winter wet.

Phlomis italica
○ ❄ ↕↕ ❖EARLY SUMMER
H 30cm (12in) S 60cm (2ft)

Less hardy than Phlomis fruticosa (above), this evergreen species has hooded, pink flowers arranged in whorls on upright, greyish-green stems in early summer. The aromatic, grey, woolly leaves provide interest at other times. It does best in a sunny spot with very well-drained soil, where it has shelter from wintry weather.

Phygelius aequalis
'Yellow Trumpet'
○ ❄ ↕↕ ❖SUMMER
H and S 90cm (3ft)

A lovely, summer-flowering evergreen that sometimes blooms into early autumn, this shrub produces its tubular, foxglove-like, pale creamy-yellow flowers on curving, upright spikes above fresh green foliage. Give it a sunny spot where it is not exposed to the worst of the winter weather.

Phygelius × rectus
'African Queen'
○ ❄ ↕↕ ❖SUMMER
H 30cm (12in) S 60cm (2ft)

Resplendent sprays of showy, tubular, pale red flowers hang from curving, upright, red spikes in summer, extending sometimes into autumn. It is a dramatic, eye-catching, evergreen shrub that will add focus to a mixed planting when other flowers start to fade. Give it a sunny, sheltered spot. Other good varieties: 'Salmon Leap' (orange flowers); 'Winchester Fanfare' (pinky-red flowers).

Pieris 'Forest Flame'
Lily-of-the-valley shrub
○ ◐ pH↓ 🍂 ❖LATE SPRING
H 4m (13ft) S 2m (6ft)

Fiery-red young leaves that turn pink, creamy white then dark green complement the pendent clusters of white flowers, reminiscent of lily-of-the-valley. It is an ideal evergreen shrub for an acidic woodland setting, or in a large tub of lime-free, ericaceous compost.

Pieris japonica
Lily-of-the-valley shrub
◐ ◖ pH↓ 🍂 ❖EARLY SPRING
H 4m (13ft) S 3m (10ft)

In early spring, this compact, evergreen shrub produces pendent sprays of white flowers like lily-of-the-valley against glossy foliage. Good varieties with pink- or red-flushed new foliage: 'Little Heath' (H and S 60cm/2ft); 'Mountain Fire' (H 3m/10ft, S 4m/13ft); 'Prelude' (H and S 2m/6ft); 'Purity' (H and S 1m/40in); 'Red Mill' (H 2m/6ft, S 1.5m/5ft). Other good varieties: 'Valley Rose' (pale pink flowers; H 1.5m/5ft, S 2m/6ft); 'Valley Valentine' (dark pink flowers).

Potentilla fruticosa
'Elizabeth' Cinquefoil
○ ◐ ⇊ ❖SUMMER
H 1m (40in) S 1.5m (5ft)

Great garden value and easy to grow, this long-flowering shrub is covered in canary-yellow flowers that look like wild roses. Use it as a border filler or grow it as an informal hedge in sun or partial shade. Other good varieties: 'Goldstar' (golden flowers); 'Pretty Polly' (pale pink flowers); 'Tangerine' (orange flowers); 'Tilford Cream' (cream flowers).

Rhododendron 'Blaauw's Pink'
○ ◐ ⇊ pH↓ 🍂 ❖LATE SPRING to EARLY SUMMER
H 80cm (32in) S 1m (40in)

Very neat and compact, this handsome, low-growing evergreen azalea would fit into any sized garden, or a pot that's filled with ericaceous compost. From late spring and into early summer it is covered in trusses of tiny, funnel-shaped, warm-pink flowers.

Rhododendron 'Blue Diamond'
○ ◐ ⇊ pH↓ 🍂 ❖LATE SPRING
H and S 1.5m (5ft)

This is a delightful, dwarf evergreen rhododendron that is smothered in trusses of funnel-shaped, bluish-purple flowers throughout late spring. The blooms fade gracefully with age. It flowers best in full sun but can tolerate dappled shade. This variety is ideal for small gardens, but needs acid soil. Alternatively, it can be grown in a tub filled with ericaceous compost.

Rhododendron 'Ginny Gee'
○ ◐ ⇊ pH↓ 🍂 ❖LATE SPRING to EARLY SUMMER
H and S 90cm (3ft)

The lovely flowers of this evergreen rhododendron are pale pinkish purple (fading to white-pink), funnel-shaped and borne in dainty trusses from late spring to early summer. The leaves are dark green and form dense mats. Very compact and low-growing, this would suit a small garden or can be grown in a tub filled with ericaceous compost.

Rhododendron 'Homebush'
○ ◐ ‡‡ pH↓ 🍃 ❖LATE SPRING
H and S 1.5m (5ft)

This is an attractive, compact and bushy deciduous azalea that bears neat trusses of funnel-shaped, bright pink, semi-double flowers during late spring. It is ideal for small gardens, but needs acid soil or can be grown in a container filled with ericaceous compost.

Rhododendron 'Kazuko' (syn. 'Geisha Red')
○ ◐ ‡‡ pH↓ 🍃 ❖LATE SPRING to EARLY SUMMER
H 60cm (2ft) S 1m (40in)

Spectacular trusses of eye-catching yet dainty, funnel-shaped, brilliant red flowers are produced on this evergreen azalea during late spring and last into early summer. Very compact and low-growing, it would fit into any sized garden, or would look good on the patio in a pot of ericaceous compost.

Rhododendrons and azaleas

There are literally thousands of different types of rhododendron, ranging from huge trees to dwarf shrubs that creep along the ground. Azaleas are just one group within the *Rhododendron* genus, and tend to be shrubby. Rhododendrons come in a huge range of colours and may be evergreen or deciduous. All need a well-drained, acid, humus-rich soil. Dwarf kinds can be grown in tubs filled with ericaceous compost.

Evergreen varieties
If you have the space and the soil, evergreen azaleas and rhododendrons make excellent shrubs for shade. They're grown for their showy, funnel-shaped flowers produced in trusses or clusters – some are so densely packed they form giant balls of colour set starkly against the dark, leathery leaves. The newer dwarf hybrids are ideal for small gardens.

All evergreen rhododendrons and azaleas are hardy.

Recommended evergreen varieties include 'Blaauw's Pink', 'Blue Diamond' and 'Ginny Gee' (*see* page 99) and 'Kazuko' (*see* left), but there are many, many others.

Deciduous azaleas
Deciduous azaleas are as hardy and flower as prolifically as evergreen rhododendrons and azaleas, but have the bonus of fabulous autumn colour. *Rhododendron luteum* is the main species (*see* opposite), but there are many garden-worthy hybrids. All have sweetly scented, colourful, funnel-shaped, late-spring flowers; the foliage is nondescript until it takes on vivid bonfire shades in autumn.

Good varieties include 'Homebush' (*see* left), the orange-flowered 'Gibraltar' and 'Klondyke', and 'Persil', with white flowers.

Rhododendrons are available in almost every flower colour, from white through pastel shades to vivid, shocking pinks.

Rhododendron luteum
○ ◑ ⬇⬇ pH⬇ 🍂
✤LATE SPRING to EARLY SUMMER, AUTUMN
H and S 4m (13ft)

This is a shaggy, deciduous azalea that bears charming, very fragrant trusses of funnel-shaped, yellow flowers from late spring into early summer. The leaves turn fiery shades in autumn. It is fairly vigorous, so takes up a lot of space in the garden. It prefers full sun and, like all rhododendrons, needs acid soil.

Rhodododendron 'Polaris'
○ ◑ ⬇⬇ pH⬇ 🍂 ✤LATE SPRING
H 1.2m (4ft) S 1m (3ft)

A floriferous evergreen rhododendron, this shrub produces masses of funnel-shaped, pinkish-purple flowers during late spring. It flowers best in full sun but can tolerate dappled shade. It is ideal for small gardens with acid soil. In gardens with an alkaline soil you can grow it in a container filled with ericaceous compost.

Rhododendron 'Unique'
○ ◑ ⬇⬇ pH⬇ 🍂 ✤LATE SPRING
H and S 1.2m (4ft)

An ideal shrub for a small garden, this compact, dense-growing, evergreen rhododendron is covered in trusses of funnel-shaped, pink and yellow tinted, ivory-white flowers. The creamy, late-spring blooms look wonderful set against the dark, bottle-green leaves. It needs acid soil, but is equally happy growing in a pot filled with ericaceous compost. It flowers best in full sun but can tolerate dappled shade.

Ribes odoratum Buffalo currant
○ ⬇⬇ ✤MID- to LATE SPRING
H and S 2m (6ft)

This is a fairly compact flowering currant that produces clove-scented, tubular, yellow flowers in pendent clusters from mid- to late spring on upright shoots. Large, rounded, black fruits follow later in the year. It is useful as a quick-growing filler or, as a group, to create an instant border in a sunny spot.

Ribes sanguineum 'Pulborough Scarlet'
Flowering currant
○ ⬇⬇ ✤LATE SPRING, SUMMER
H 3m (10ft) S 2.5m (8ft)

Stalwart of the spring garden, the flowering currant is reliable and easy to grow, producing pendent clusters of deep-red, tubular flowers followed by spherical, blue-black berries later in the year. Unfortunately, the flowers are short-lived and at other times the shrub is a little dull. Other good varieties: 'King Edward VII' (crimson flowers).

Rosmarinus officinalis
Rosemary
○ ❄ ◌ ⬇⬇ ✤SPRING to SUMMER
H and S 1.5m (5ft)

Delightfully aromatic, needle-like, dark green leaves clothe upright spikes that are encrusted with endearingly scruffy, purple-blue flowers from mid-spring into summer. Use it in the border or as an informal evergreen hedge. Good varieties: 'Majorca Pink' (pale pink flowers; H and S 1m/40in); 'Miss Jessopp's Upright' (purple-blue flowers; H and S 2m/6ft); 'Roseus' (pink flowers).

Salix hastata 'Wehrhahnii'
◯ ◌ ↕ ❖EARLY SPRING
H and S 1m (40in)

A compact and slow-growing shrub, this has attractive, dark purple-brown shoots that contrast with the eye-catching silvery catkins, 8cm (3in) long, borne in early spring and followed by saw-edged, fresh green foliage.

Sambucus nigra 'Gerda'
Black elder
◯ ◐ ◌ ↕ ❖EARLY SUMMER, AUTUMN
H and S 3m (10ft)

Formerly known as 'Black Beauty', this bears lovely, lemon-scented, pale pink flowers opening from red buds in early summer, followed by purple fruits. But it is the purple-black foliage that is the main feature, making this elder a perfect filler. It retains its colour best in dappled shade. Another good variety: 'Eva' (formerly 'Black Lace'; deeply cut purple foliage turns black in shade; S 2m/6ft).

Sambucus racemosa 'Sutherland Gold' Red-berried elder
◐ ◌ ↕ ❖SPRING, SUMMER
H and S 3m (10ft)

Creamy spring flowers followed by glossy red fruits are attractive enough, but the main feature of this decorative elder is the stunning, finely cut foliage on arching stems that emerges bronze before turning a glorious golden colour. Ideally, plant it in partial shade, since the foliage can scorch in full sun. It is an ideal choice for planting in the back of a mixed border.

Santolina chamaecyparissus 'Nana' Cotton lavender
◯ ❄ ◌ ↕ ❖LATE SUMMER
H 30cm (12in) S 45cm (18in)

Sunny, button-like flowers embellish a dense, silvery mound of delicate, evergreen, aromatic leaves. This compact variety can be used at the front of a sheltered, sunny border, or will make a shaggy, cloud-like, informal low hedge provided it is protected from cold winds. Another good variety: 'Lambrook Silver' (lemon-yellow flowers).

Sarcococca confusa
Christmas box
◐ ◐ ◌ ↕ ❖LATE WINTER
H 2m (6ft) S 1m (40in)

Gorgeously scented, snow-white, late-winter flowers shine out against the glossy, dark green foliage of this dense, evergreen shrub. Rounded, glossy black fruits follow. It is particularly useful in really tough areas of deep shade, such as on the north side of evergreen hedges and between buildings.

Sarcococca hookeriana var. digyna Christmas box
◐ ● ❄ ◌ ↕ ❖LATE WINTER
H 1.5m (5ft) S 2m (6ft)

Fragile-looking, vanilla-scented, mauve-tinted white flowers hang tassel-like in clusters during late winter, set off by the bottle-green foliage of this compact, multi-stemmed, evergreen shrub. Round, glossy black fruits follow. It is ideal for winter interest in a border in shade, or, to appreciate the delightful fragrance to the full, place it near a well-used shady path or entrance.

Skimmia × confusa 'Kew Green'

◐ ○ ◖ ♦ ‡‡ ❖LATE SPRING
H 3m (10ft) S 1.5m (5ft)

This subtle and underrated green-budded skimmia forms a neat, dome shaped, evergreen shrub that reveals its dense clusters of fragrant, creamy-white flowers in late spring. Ideal for shade, it is an excellent filler that accentuates cool colour schemes, and is especially useful for adding light to shady borders and as a pollinator for female skimmia varieties.

Skimmia japonica
Japanese skimmia

◐ ○ ◖ ‡‡ ✤ ❖SPRING, WINTER
H and S 1.5m (5ft)

Compact and ideal for containers, with a long season of interest, this evergreen shrub has dense clusters of fragrant, white or pink-tinted, spring flowers opening from red buds and, on female plants, stunning crops of red fruits that last all winter. To ensure fruit, plant both male and female, or a hermaphrodite. Good varieties: 'Fragrans' (m); subsp. *reevesiana* (hermaphrodite); 'Nymans' (f); 'Rubella' (m); 'Veitchii' (f).

Sophora 'Sun King'

○ ‡‡ ❖LATE SPRING
H and S 3m (10ft)

Large, bell-shaped, butter-yellow flowers hang from arching branches on this open, spreading, evergreen shrub during late spring. The flowers are long-lasting and eye-catching, but the shrub can look a bit tatty once the petals fall. It is a good, unusual choice for a sunny border. Alternatively, it can be trained against a warm wall or fence.

Sorbaria kirilowii Tree spiraea

○ ◐ ◖ ‡‡ pH→ -pH↑ ❖MID- to LATE SUMMER
H 3m (10ft) S 4m (13ft)

This attractive shrub has elegant, divided foliage on arching shoots and frothy, white, flowering plumes, up to 40cm (16in) long, from midsummer. It is good for a large border or waterside planting, but is vigorous and can be invasive.

Spartium junceum
Spanish broom

○ ‡‡ ❖EARLY SUMMER to EARLY AUTUMN
H and S 3m (10ft)

From early summer, the bright green, rush-like stems of Spanish broom are covered in a succession of fragrant, sunshine-yellow, pea-shaped flowers. Easy to grow, this open, spiky shrub is a good choice for a gravel garden and, being salt-tolerant, it can be grown in coastal gardens too.

Spiraea 'Arguta' Bridal wreath

○ ‡‡ ❖MID-SPRING
H and S 2.5m (8ft)

This easy-to-grow shrub is deservedly popular for its graceful, arching stems that carry foaming clusters of tiny, white flowers in mid-spring. Useful as a filler for a sunny shrub border, it would also make an excellent backdrop in a mixed border.

Spiraea japonica 'Anthony Waterer'

○ ⬇⬇ ❖SUMMER
H and S 1.5m (5ft)

Glorious, crimson-pink flowers are produced in flat heads from midsummer above mounds of attractive, saw-edged, cream-variegated foliage. The leaves emerge bronze-red and turn dark green. Grow in a sunny mixed border or a shrub border, or as an eye-catching informal, flowering hedge. Other good varieties: 'Little Princess' (pale pink flowers; H 50cm/20in, S 1m/40in); 'Genpei' ('Shirobana') (deep-pink and white flowers; H and S 60cm/2ft).

Spiraea nipponica 'Snowmound'

○ ⬇⬇ ❖EARLY SUMMER
H and S 2.5m (8ft)

Upright when young but becoming spreading as it matures, this lovely shrub bears foaming clusters of tiny, white flowers on slender, arching stems in early summer. Plant in a sunny border.

Spiraea thunbergii

○ ⬇⬇ ❖SPRING to EARLY SUMMER, AUTUMN
H 1.5m (5ft) S 2m (6ft)

Shaggy and bushy, this deciduous or semi-evergreen, early-flowering shrub produces foaming clusters of tiny, white flowers on wiry stems from mid-spring. The slightly toothed, fresh green leaves turn yellow in autumn. It is a good filler shrub for a sunny border.

Spiraea × vanhouttei

○ ◗ ❖EARLY SUMMER
H 2m (6ft) S 1.5m (5ft)

The gracefully arching branches of this bushy and compact shrub are covered in foaming clusters of tiny, white flowers from early summer. The attractive, diamond-shaped, saw-edged dark green leaves have a bluish sheen underneath. Plant in a sunny border, beside water, or as an informal, flowering hedge.

Syringa meyeri 'Palibin'
Korean lilac

○ ⬇⬇ pH➔–pH↑ ❖LATE SPRING to EARLY SUMMER
H 2m (6ft) S 1.5m (5ft)

Perhaps the best lilac for smaller gardens, this bears superbly fragrant conical clusters, 10cm (4in) long, of lilac-pink flowers from late spring into early summer. Coping well with alkaline soil, it is a good choice for new gardens strewn with builders' rubble.

Syringa × persica Persian lilac

○ ⬇⬇ pH➔–pH↑ ❖LATE SPRING to EARLY SUMMER
H and S 2m (6ft)

Useful where space is at a premium, this lilac forms a neat shrub reaching just waist-height after five years and doubling this size at maturity. In late spring, it is covered in conical clusters of delightfully fragrant, purple flowers.

Syringa pubescens subsp. microphylla 'Superba'

○ ↓↓ pH►–pH↑ ❖LATE SPRING to SUMMER
H and S 6m (20ft)

A little more compact than the common lilac, this variety bears superbly fragrant, conical clusters of rose-pink flowers during late spring and then on and off through summer. You can use it towards the back of a shrub border or mixed border, as an informal flowering hedge, or even trained on wires against a wall.

Syringa vulgaris Common lilac

○ ↓↓ pH►–pH↑ ❖EARLY SUMMER
H and S 7m (23ft)

Deliciously fragrant, conical clusters of single or double flowers, in various shades of purple, mauve, pink and white, are produced in early summer on this tree-like shrub. Good varieties: 'Charles Joly' (dark purple-red flowers; shown above); 'Katherine Havemeyer' (lavender-blue flowers); 'Madame Lemoine' (white flowers); 'Michel Buchner' (rose flowers).

Teucrium fruticans
Shrubby germander

○ ✳ ↓↓ pH►–pH↑ ❖EARLY SUMMER
H 60cm (2ft) S 4m (13ft)

Whorls of sky-blue summer flowers complement the aromatic, grey-green foliage on this bushy, evergreen shrub. Coping well with alkaline soil, it is a good choice for new gardens where builders' rubble lurks beneath the surface, as long as the soil is well drained and the garden is sheltered.

Thymus serpyllum 'Pink Chintz'
Thyme

○ ◊ ↓↓ pH►–pH↑ ❖EARLY SUMMER
H 25cm (10in) S 45cm (18in)

Delightful, bright pink flowers are produced en masse in early summer on this low-growing, shrubby thyme. It makes a good evergreen edging plant or ground cover for a sunny border, or it can be grown between cracks in paving, where its aromatic grey-green leaves will release their soothing scent when lightly crushed underfoot. Another good variety: var. albus (white flowers).

Thymus vulgaris Garden thyme

○ ◊ ↓↓ pH►–pH↑ ❖LATE SPRING to EARLY SUMMER
H 30cm (12in) S 40cm (16in)

Popular and widely cultivated, garden thyme is often one of the first herbs grown by beginner gardeners. It is a ground-hugging, bushy, evergreen shrub, with delicate, white to purple flowers from late spring. The leaves are used in various dishes, and stems can be dried for making bouquets garnis.

Ulex europaeus Gorse

○ ↓↓ ❖SPRING
H 2.5m (8ft) S 2m (6ft)

Impenetrable, spine-tipped, evergreen shoots make this upright, dense gorse an ideal perimeter shrub where you want to deter intruders. In spring it becomes a beacon of sunny-yellow flowers that have a distinct coconut fragrance. A light sprinkling of blooms is produced intermittently at other times. Good variety: 'Flore Pleno' (semi-double, yellow flowers).

Viburnum × *bodnantense* 'Charles Lamont'
○ ◑ ◐ 💧 ‡‡ ❖WINTER to SPRING
H 3m (10ft) S 2m (6ft)

Fresh pink, waxy-looking, fragrant flowers are borne in dense clusters on bare stems from early winter until mid-spring. An upright shrub that is clothed in saw-edged, dark green foliage, it makes an unassuming backdrop for other plants the rest of the year. Plant next to a sheltered path or entrance. Another good variety: 'Dawn' (dark pink flowers).

Viburnum × *burkwoodii* 'Anne Russell'
○ ◑ ◐ 💧 ‡‡ ❖LATE SPRING, AUTUMN
H 2m (6ft) S 1.5m (5ft)

This adorable, compact, rounded shrub is an excellent choice where space is limited in the garden. During late spring it bears fragrant clusters of snow-white flowers that open from pink buds. The polished dark foliage takes on colourful autumn tints too.

Viburnum carlesii
Korean spice viburnum
○ ◑ ◐ 💧 ‡‡ ❖LATE SPRING, AUTUMN
H and S 2m (6ft)

This thickly growing viburnum bears tight clusters of pink buds that open into balls of deliciously fragrant, white or pink-flushed, late-spring flowers. The toothed, dark green foliage turns red-purple in autumn. It is ideal in a mixed border or shrub border – plant it next to a path to fully appreciate the lovely scent. Good variety: 'Aurora' (red buds open pink; shown above).

Viburnum davidii
○ ◑ ◐ 💧 ‡‡ ❖LATE SPRING, AUTUMN to WINTER
H and S 1.5m (5ft)

Stunning, metallic-looking, turquoise, bead-like fruits on coral-red stalks follow flattened heads of white spring flowers and are the highlight of this evergreen viburnum. At other times, the handsome, veined, dark green leaves are an excellent foil for other plants. Reliable and easy to grow, it makes an excellent front-of-the-border filler and winter-interest ground-cover shrub.

Viburnum 'Eskimo'
○ ◑ ◐ 💧 ‡‡ ❖LATE SPRING
H and S 1.5m (5ft)

A compact, semi-evergreen shrub, this viburnum bears snowball-like, rounded clusters of pink-flushed buds that open to reveal snow-white, tubular flowers in late spring. It is an excellent front-of-border, hummock-forming shrub that contrasts well with more upright plants.

Viburnum farreri
○ ◑ ◐ 💧 ‡‡ ❖WINTER to SPRING
H 3m (10ft) S 2.5m (8ft)

This is an excellent winter-flowering viburnum, bearing dense clusters of fragrant, white or pink-tinted flowers that open on bare stems from pink buds. The flowers are sometimes followed by bright red fruits. It is ideal in a mixed border, in sun or partial shade, sheltered from cold winds.

Viburnum × *juddii*
○ ◑ ● ♦ ‡‡ ❖LATE SPRING
H 1.2m (4ft) S 1.5m (5ft)

This is a lovely viburnum, laden in late spring with tight clusters of pink buds that open into balls of fragrant, pink-flushed white flowers. The oval, dark green foliage sometimes turns red in autumn, too. It is more aphid-proof than some viburnums.

Viburnum opulus 'Compactum'
Guelder rose
○ ◑ ♦ ❖EARLY SUMMER, AUTUMN
H and S 1.5m (5ft)

Stunning, fiery bonfire shades in autumn are the main feature of this compact viburnum, although the white lacecap, early-summer flowers and the bright red fruits that follow are attractive too. It is ideal for a wildlife area or a woodland-edge planting. Another good variety: 'Roseum' (white or green-tinged white flowers; H and S 3m/10ft).

Viburnum plicatum f. *tomentosum* 'Mariesii'
Japanese snowball bush
○ ◑ ● ♦ ‡‡ ❖LATE SPRING
H 3m (10ft) S 4m (13ft)

A beautiful, horizontally tiered shrub, the Japanese snowball bush bears white, lacecap, late-spring flowers that age gracefully to pink. The deeply veined leaves turn red-purple in autumn. It is ideal at the back of a mixed border in sun or partial shade. Other good varieties: 'Pink Beauty' (white flowers turn pink); 'Summer Snowflake' (flowers to early autumn, H 2.5m/8ft, S 1.5m/5ft).

Viburnum tinus Laurustinus
○ ◑ ● ♦ ☘ ❀ ❖EARLY WINTER to SPRING
H and S 3m (10ft)

Stalwart of the shady border, this conical, evergreen shrub bears flat heads of white flowers from early winter to spring, then blue-black fruits. It is reliable, easy and a fine winter-interest shrub. Good varieties: 'Eve Price' (pink buds, pinkish-white flowers); 'French White' (pink buds, white flowers); 'Gwenllian' (dark pink buds, pinkish-white flowers; shown above); 'Variegatum' (leaves edged pale yellow).

Weigela 'Bristol Ruby'
○ ◑ ♦ ‡‡ ❖EARLY SUMMER
H 2.5m (8ft) S 2m (6ft)

Clusters of bell-shaped, ruby-red flowers open from purplish-red buds in early summer on this vigorous, upright shrub. Easy to grow, it is a good choice for new gardens where space is limited. Other good varieties: 'Abel Carrière' (deep-pink flowers; H and S 2m/6ft); 'Minuet' (dark pink flowers; H 75cm/30in, S 1.2m/4ft); 'Snowflake' (snow-white flowers; H 1.2m/4ft, S 1.5m/5ft); 'Victoria' (deep rose-pink flowers; H and S 1.5m/5ft).

Weigela florida 'Foliis Purpureis'
○ ◑ ♦ ‡‡ ❖EARLY SUMMER
H and S 2.5m (8ft)

Funnel-shaped, dark pink flowers are produced in little fanfares on gracefully arching stems with bronze-flushed foliage. Being compact, it is ideal for a mixed border, in sun or partial shade, where space is at a premium.

Shrubs for challenging sites

Generally, flowering shrubs are pretty tolerant of their growing conditions, but there are some situations that are particularly challenging. As is the case with any plant, a shrub planted in the wrong place can result in poor growth, lack of flowers and increased susceptibility to pest and disease attack. Fortunately, however, there are flowering shrubs that are well adapted to cope with almost any given situation, so by choosing carefully you'll have healthy, thriving plants that transform difficult areas into attractive places.

Dense shade

Deep, permanent shade found on the north side of buildings and garden structures, and under large evergreen trees, is perhaps the most challenging site for flowering shrubs. Don't despair: there are some choice plants that will succeed – and one or two other ways of brightening the gloom.

The shady stalwarts

Mahonias are superb flowering shrubs for heavy shade. These bold, evergreen plants are loved for their bright yellow, fragrant flowers in winter, held like oversized bunches of lily-of-the-valley above dramatic foliage. Plant a variety such as *Mahonia × media* 'Charity' alongside the variegated Ivy *Hedera colchica* 'Sulphur Heart' or *Euonymus fortunei* 'Emerald 'n' Gold', whose foliage will continue the yellow theme all year.

Skimmia japonica is a smaller-growing evergreen for full shade. In fact, sun tends to make its leaves turn yellow. White flowers open in spring, and some varieties have red berries in winter. Other shade-tolerant evergreens include the dwarf Christmas box (*Sarcococca*

Plant both male and female forms of the shade-loving *Skimmia japonica* to produce reliable crops of berries.

confusa), with small, highly scented white winter flowers, and the tough *Viburnum tinus*, with white flowers from early winter to spring.

In an area riddled with the roots of a tree or a hedge, or close to a tree trunk, it would be better to consider using shrubs in containers rather than planting them in the open ground.

Adding colour and light

As the number of flowering shrubs suitable for dense shade is limited, you should also think of using foliage to add colour and light. Good foliage plants are the spotted laurel (*Aucuba japonica*), variegated ivies

(used as ground cover and on walls and fences) and the glossy, light-reflecting *Fatsia japonica*.

To some extent, you can alleviate the problems of dense shade under a large tree by pruning overhanging branches – but you might have to repeat the process every few years.

You can increase the amount of light reaching plants in the shadow of buildings and fences by painting them with a light-reflecting paint or wood stain. Pale-coloured paving or gravel also makes a big difference.

More shrubs for dense shade

Camellia japonica 'Alba Simplex'
Daphne pontica
Mahonia aquifolium 'Smaragd'
Rhododendron 'Cunningham's White'
Sarcococca hookeriana var. *digyna*
Viburnum davidii
Vinca minor 'Argenteovariegata'

Steep slopes and banks

Steep slopes and banks are often tricky to plant up and maintain. They can be difficult to access for weeding and any general tidying up, and the soil is often dry. However, once established, low-spreading flowering shrubs provide excellent ground cover, and little maintenance will be required. The effect can be attractive; a change in level makes the garden more interesting and plants are shown off to advantage.

Choosing plants

In a sunny site, *Ceanothus thyrsiflorus* var. *repens*, with its arching stems, dark green leaves and bright blue flowers, is unbeatable cascading down a bank. *Genista lydia* may seem garish to some, but it does inject a shot of sunshine into a scheme; you could soften the bright yellow flowers by partnering it with the silver-grey foliage of the cotton lavender *Santolina chamaecyparissus* 'Nana'.

Planted on a sunny bank, the broom *Genista lydia* will spread up to a metre wide, forming a mass of canary-yellow flowers during early summer.

More shrubs for steep slopes and banks

SUNNY SLOPES

Berberis thunbergii f. *atropurpurea* 'Atropurpurea Nana'

Ceanothus griseus var. *horizontalis* 'Yankee Point'

Hebe pinguifolia 'Pagei'

SLOPES IN PARTIAL SHADE

Cotoneaster dammeri

Gaultheria procumbens

Mahonia aquifolium 'Apollo'

Vinca minor 'Argenteovariegata'

All varieties of the rock rose, *Helianthemum*, form low mats of dark green or grey evergreen foliage; single or double, red, yellow, orange, pink or white flowers appear over several weeks in early summer. You just need to clip the plants after flowering to keep them compact.

Periwinkles are an obvious choice for slopes in sun or shade. *Vinca minor* 'La Grave' has evergreen leaves and a mass of sky-blue flowers over a long period in spring and summer. *Vinca minor* 'Illumination' has the bonus of bright gold and green variegated foliage, too; it really livens up a shady slope. To extend the flowering season, plant with dwarf bulbs such as *Narcissus* 'February Gold' and *Chionodoxa luciliae*.

On neutral or acid soils, heaths and heathers are useful for ground cover on slopes and banks: the more spreading varieties of *Erica carnea* and *Calluna vulgaris* work well if you can give them a light clip over after flowering to promote bushy growth. *Erica carnea* 'Springwood White' is a good variety, with strong, trailing growth and plentiful flowers. As long as the soil is not too dry, you could combine these with a low-spreading azalea, for example *Rhododendron* 'Kermesinum', which has vivid purple-red flowers and small, dark green leaves.

Hot, dry spots

Most gardens have at least one hot, dry spot that needs careful planting, often along a south-facing wall or fence. The secret is to choose plants that prefer a site like this and to treat sunny, dry areas as an opportunity to grow some of our favourite plants – and this includes many less-than-hardy shrubs, as well as aromatics from Mediterranean regions.

Plants for hot, dry areas

Drought-tolerant flowering shrubs are the obvious starting point for a hot, dry spot. Many of these have adaptations to reduce water loss – look for leaves that are silver, small, and leathery or hairy.

Lavender and cotton lavender (*Santolina*), both silver-leaved plants, revel in dry conditions and hate winter wet. The California lilacs are also well adapted. Varieties such as

Romneya coulteri will thrive in a hot spot at the foot of a south-facing wall. This will give it the protection it needs in a severe winter.

Ceanothus 'Puget Blue' and 'Concha' will grow well as freestanding subjects or in dry, narrow borders against sunny walls or fences. *Fremontodendron californicum* is another ideal shrub for a high, south-facing wall or fence, producing large, golden, cup-shaped flowers from spring to autumn. The pineapple broom (*Cytisus battandieri*), with its silky, silver, felted leaves, is well suited to arid conditions and, given plenty of sun, will grow vigorously and produce plentiful yellow pineapple-scented flowers in midsummer.

The crimson bottlebrush (*Callistemon citrinus* 'Splendens') has proved to be a garden favourite in cooler climates, provided it has a sheltered, sunny situation in the garden. Its narrow, leathery leaves make it extremely drought-tolerant and it will reward with a spectacular display of fluffy, scarlet flowers in spring and summer.

When you can't decide what to plant in a hot, dry situation always opt for a sun rose (*Cistus*). They are easy-care shrubs that flower freely and reliably from early summer. The white *Cistus obtusifolius* 'Thrive' and bright cerise *Cistus* × *pulverulentus* 'Sunset' are two of the best, with flowers throughout the summer.

Growing tips

Even the most drought-tolerant shrubs need a little extra care in the early stages. Planting in autumn is ideal, because the soil is warm and moist. You might need to protect tender plants such as *Abutilon* and *Coronilla* in winter (*see* page 59). It helps to add a gravel mulch after planting. This reflects light back onto the plants and keeps winter wet off leaves and stems.

More shrubs for hot, dry spots

Abutilon × *suntense* 'Jermyns'
Berberis darwinii
Buddleja 'Lochinch'
Bupleurum fruticosum
Cistus 'Elma'
Coronilla valentina subsp. *glauca* 'Citrina'
Escallonia 'Apple Blossom'
Genista hispanica
Helianthemum nummularium
Lavandula angustifolia
Olearia × *haastii*
Phlomis italica
Rosmarinus officinalis
Spartium junceum
Teucrium fruticans

Sandy soil

Sandy soils are usually well drained but low in fertility, because rainwater passes straight through taking any water-soluble nutrients with it. These soils dry out quickly. In winter this is a plus point, because you can dig almost immediately after rainfall, but in summer they can be a bit too dry. Shrubs soon adapt and their roots go deep in search of water, meaning they suffer less in dry weather than plants that grow on more moisture-retentive soil.

Lavender is drought-tolerant and well adapted to sandy ground.

Choosing your shrubs

Sandy soils are often acidic, so heaths and heathers do well. Tree heaths are well worth considering. *Erica arborea* var. *alpina* is the best, with bright green foliage and white flowers in spring. It grows to 2m (6ft), and mixes well with evergreen shrubs, heathers and conifers.

Whether the soil is acid or alkaline, plants with grey foliage, such as lavender and cotton lavender (*Santolina*), will live longer than when on heavy, moist soils. *Convolvulus cneorum*, with its silky silver leaves, is an ideal dwarf shrub for a hot, dry spot. Shrubs with aromatic foliage, like rosemary and thyme, can also be relied upon.

The brooms grow quickly and reward with prolific, spicily scented flowers in spring. *Cytisus* × *praecox*, with its pale, creamy-yellow flowers, is a good mixer and lovely planted with an early-flowering California lilac such as *Ceanothus* 'Puget Blue'. Brooms get leggy with age; prevent this by trimming them over when young, straight after flowering.

Most hebes find sandy soils too dry, but small-leaved varieties with grey leaves will succeed. *Hebe* 'Red Edge' is tough and the best choice for a low, dome-shaped shrub.

Improving sandy soils

The best way to improve sandy soils is to apply bulky organic matter such as well-rotted farmyard manure or garden compost. Dig it into the soil when preparing for planting. As well as mulching, you should feed your shrubs with a slow-release fertilizer when you plant them, and feed again each spring. Rose fertilizer is ideal for all flowering shrubs except lime-haters (those that like acid soil). Plants may need a little extra care after planting, until the roots are established, so do water regularly.

More shrubs for sandy soil

Abelia × *grandiflora*
Abutilon × *suntense* 'Jermyns'
Callistemon citrinus 'Splendens'
Corokia cotoneaster
Cytisus 'Minstead'
Genista lydia
× *Halimiocistus* 'Ingwersenii'
Olearia macrodonta
Perovskia 'Blue Spire'
Romneya coulteri
Rosmarinus officinalis
Santolina chamaecyparissus 'Nana'
Spartium junceum

Clay soil

Gardeners hate clay soils, because they are heavy, wet in winter and difficult to work with. However, they are moisture-retentive and fertile, so most flowering shrubs love them. Many of the familiar old favourites grow on clay soils, so you have plenty to choose from to give continuity of interest throughout the year.

Making the right choice

Clay soils can be alkaline or acid, so it's worth checking the pH of yours before choosing plants. If it's acid, you can grow azaleas, magnolias and other fine shrubs (*see* page 116).

Forsythias love clay and make a welcome show in early spring. *Forsythia* × *intermedia* 'Week-End' is more compact than most, a good choice for small gardens. Blooming at the same time, the flowering currant (*Ribes sanguineum*) is reliable and has aromatic foliage. If you don't like its pinkish-red flowers, opt for a more subtle variety, such as 'White Icicle'.

Viburnums are very accommodating flowering shrubs, tolerating a wide range of soils, even heavy clay, when grown in either sun or shade.

More shrubs for clay soil

Chaenomeles × *superba* 'Crimson and Gold'
Choisya ternata
Hydrangea paniculata 'Unique'
Hypericum 'Hidcote'
Kerria japonica 'Pleniflora'
Mahonia × *media* 'Charity'
Osmanthus delavayi
Philadelphus 'Virginal'
Spiraea japonica 'Anthony Waterer'
Weigela 'Kosteriana Variegata'

Cotoneasters are dependable shrubs offering spring flowers and winter berries. They grow in sun or shade and thrive on even the most inhospitable clay. *Cotoneaster franchetii* is a good mixer, with a pleasing arching habit and semi-evergreen, grey-green foliage.

Viburnums thrive on clay, from the reliable evergreen *Viburnum tinus* to the stately, showy *Viburnum plicatum* f. *tomentosum* 'Mariesii'. This makes a fine freestanding specimen or focal point at the corner of a bed. It needs space to develop its layered horizontal branches, which carry lacecap heads of white flowers in late spring.

Improving clay soils

Before planting, improve the structure and drainage of clay soils by digging and forking over the soil. If you do this in autumn, prior to planting in spring, the weathering effects of winter frosts will help to open up the soil structure. Work in plenty of bulky organic matter – the more, the better! On heavy clay soils, add grit to help improve the surface drainage.

When planting, dig a nice big hole and break up the surrounding soil. Add plenty of compost to encourage the plant's roots to venture out into the clay.

FOCUS ON | Wind tunnels and frost pockets

The growing environment in your garden is determined by a range of factors – where you live and at what altitude, as well as how exposed your garden is to the prevailing wind, will largely dictate the conditions. However, local factors, such as whether you live in an urban area or near the coast, will also have an influence. Even within the same garden you'll find a range of varying microclimates. The areas covered by a particular microclimate can be very small – where cold air is trapped against a wall or fence creating a frost pocket, for example, or within a passageway where a turbulent wind tunnel is caused by nearby buildings.

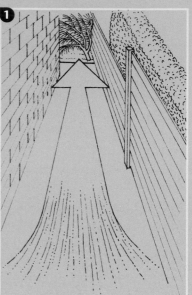

Wind tunnels

In urban areas, the effects of wind can be exacerbated by the surrounding buildings, which create damaging turbulence and can funnel the wind, making it stronger. The detrimental effect of wind is more than just a few broken and bruised stems: even the slightest breeze slows growth and reduces the chances of the shrub flowering, because the wind increases moisture loss and reduces temperatures.

The moisture loss from leaves and stems, as well as from the soil surface, causes particular problems with flowering shrubs that are growing in dry soil between buildings. Just as in an exposed garden, you can reduce the wind speed in a wind tunnel between buildings by planting a 'shelter belt' of wind-tolerant shrubs, such as spotted laurel (*Aucuba japonica*) or varieties of *Berberis darwinii* and *Berberis × stenophylla*. This may mean creating a small border at one end of the passage to slow the wind and cut down on turbulence. Put up a windbreak after planting, to help protect shrubs as they are getting established; this is particularly important for evergreens and not-so-hardy plants.

Mulch all plants to help reduce water loss from the soil (*see* page 58) and, because diseases are transferred more readily in the wind, keep up with pruning tasks (*see* pages 60–5).

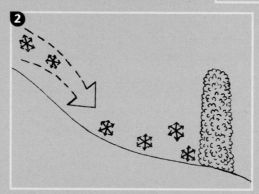

It is best to avoid planting in certain parts of the garden. ① It is often assumed that town gardens are sheltered, but passageways between buildings and fences can create wind tunnels, which can be damaging to plants. ② Cold air often collects at the lowest point in the garden, so avoid planting at the bottom of a slope if possible. If the barrier is a hedge, you could trim it to leave a small space for air to flow out.

Frost pockets

Look at your garden on a frosty morning and you will be able to see any parts that have trapped cold air. If your garden slopes down to a fence, the most likely place will be at the lowest point, by the fence. Although frost pockets usually occur in front of solid barriers such as walls and fences that trap cold air as it moves down a slope, hedges and borders filled with shrubs can also trap cold air.

The solution is to provide an exit for the cold air. This can be as simple as leaving gaps at the bottom of a barrier so cold air can escape through the gaps rather than collecting at the base.

Where it is not possible to do away with a frost pocket, choose plants that are very frost-resistant, and avoid any hardy plants that leaf-up early and are prone to leaf scorch, such as hydrangeas. Planting for shelter on the north and east sides of your garden will help to reduce the effects of damaging frost pockets. Take steps during the winter months to protect shrubs planted in a frost pocket by covering the soil with an insulating mulch of dry leaves or bracken.

Wet conditions

Deep, well-drained, fertile soil that never dries out provides the ultimate growing conditions. If you're lucky enough to have it, you can grow almost anything. On the other hand if your soil is permanently wet, perhaps waterlogged in winter, you have to be selective in your choice of flowering shrubs. Opt for those that thrive in these damp conditions and use them to make stunning combinations with moisture-loving perennials such as *Gunnera, Ligularia, Rodgersia, Iris sibirica* and *Lythrum*.

Moisture-loving shrubs

Mophead and lacecap hydrangeas grow well in damp conditions, especially in semi-shade. In frost pockets, new growth can be damaged in early spring, but the plants recover later in the season. There are many good varieties of *Hydrangea macrophylla* in shades of red, pink and white. On acid soil, many red and pink varieties produce blue, mauve or purple blooms (*see* page 29). Look out for *Hydrangea* 'Zorro', with dark stems and lacecap flowers of sapphire blue (mauve on alkaline soil).

The Himalayan honeysuckle (*Leycesteria formosa*) is one of the easiest shrubs to grow and thrives in wet soil. It is particularly attractive by water, where the arching green stems can overhang the edge and show off the hanging purple flowers

With wet soil, take the opportunity to set flowering shrubs like *Hydrangea macrophylla* against the big, bold foliage of *Gunnera manicata*.

well. The stems look good in winter alongside those of *Cornus alba*.

There are many attractive elders that grow well in wet conditions. The cut-leaved elder, *Sambucus nigra* f. *laciniata*, is a big shrub with feathery foliage and flat heads of white flowers in summer, followed by red-black fruits. All elders, including the purple, yellow and variegated forms, benefit from hard pruning in late winter in their early years to stimulate vigorous growth.

Planting in moist soils

Where the ground remains wet for long periods, avoid planting in late autumn or winter. The soil will be cold and hard to work and could very easily compact. Water might collect in the planting hole, suffocating the plant's roots. Plant in late spring or early summer instead, when the soil will be warmer and easier to work. Add plenty of well-rotted organic matter to the planting hole and the surrounding soil, in order to give your new plant the best possible start.

More shrubs for wet conditions

Amelanchier lamarckii
Andromeda polifolia
Clethra alnifolia
Sorbaria tomentosa
Spiraea × vanhouttei
Viburnum opulus

Acidic soil

If you have acidic soil you can grow all those wonderful shrubs that gardeners admire: magnolias, rhododendrons, azaleas and camellias. The spectacle might make your garden focused on spring, but it's always worth waiting for. However, acid soils range from light and sandy to heavy clay and you need to take this into account when choosing what to plant in your garden.

Plants for acidic soil

Acidic clay soils are more fertile than sandy ones; they also retain water better. First choice, if you have room, is *Magnolia* × *soulangeana*. A mature plant covered in those great, waxy, pink and white goblets is a glorious sight in spring. Don't plant it in an open, windy site as the blooms are easily damaged; and be prepared for the odd hard frost that kills the flowers. Give this plant space, as it is spoilt by bad pruning. For smaller gardens, choose *Magnolia liliiflora* 'Nigra', with purple-red flowers, or lipstick-pink *Magnolia* 'Susan'.

The magnificent, wide-spreading *Magnolia* × *soulangeana* prefers a slightly acidic soil and makes an excellent specimen plant for a large lawn.

More shrubs for acidic soil

Cornus kousa var. *chinensis*
Corylopsis pauciflora
Desfontainia spinosa
Embothrium coccineum
Enkianthus campanulatus
Eucryphia × *nymansensis* 'Nymansay'
Hamamelis × *intermedia* 'Pallida'
Kalmia latifolia
Pieris 'Forest Flame'

Many rhododendrons are good options for acidic clay soil (*see* pages 99–101). Two impressive varieties include 'Nova Zembla', with crimson flowers in mid-spring, and 'Mrs Furnivall', covered in trusses of pink flowers in late spring. Both reach up to 3m (10ft) high. Don't be put off by the ultimate size of the larger rhododendrons; they can be cut back after flowering to control size.

Camellias are good on reasonably moist acidic soils, but are best planted where the morning sun can't spoil the flowers after a frost. *Camellia japonica* varieties have broad, glossy, dark green leaves on mostly compact plants. For a lighter effect, *Camellia* × *williamsii* 'Donation', with a more open habit and soft-pink flowers, takes some beating.

On drier acid soils, such as sand and gravel, make the most of the heathers and heaths (*see* page 80). By choosing a range of *Calluna*, *Erica* and *Daboecia* varieties, you can have flower and foliage interest all year. They make great partners for azaleas and dwarf rhododendrons.

Planting on acidic soil

Acidic clay soils and light, sandy and stony soils can be improved by adding organic matter. Acid-loving plants are light feeders, so don't mind that these soils are low in nutrients. Feed annually with a slow-release ericaceous fertilizer.

Chalky soil

Soils that overlay chalk or limestone tend to be thin and dry; the porous bedrock allows rain to drain away quickly, taking nutrients with it. Nevertheless, there is a host of flowering shrubs that revel in chalky conditions, including some of our most loved plants. And if you crave rhododendrons and azaleas, you can always grow them in pots of ericaceous compost.

Plants for alkaline soil

Many shrubby herbs originate from areas with dry, chalky soil. So a rosemary such as *Rosmarinus officinalis* 'Miss Jessopp's Upright' will thrive, bearing early blue flowers as a bonus to the aromatic foliage. Thymes, such as *Thymus serpyllum* 'Pink Chintz', form low mounds or mats of aromatic foliage and fragrant flowers in summer – ideal for softening paving or planting in gravel.

Buddleias thrive on the shallowest of chalk soils and are useful for their late-summer flowers. Some varieties of *Buddleja davidii* grow to 4m (13ft) or more. For a smaller garden, opt for 'Nanho Purple' and similar varieties less than half that size.

Fuchsias succeed on chalk in sun or shade. 'Genii' grows to 60cm (2ft), with yellow leaves and red and blue flowers. The slender 'Riccartonii' makes a reliable large shrub on chalky soil, and a good hedge in mild areas. Plant it with *Deutzia*, mock orange (*Philadelphus*), *Weigela* or lilac (*Syringa*), all of which thrive in these conditions, to extend the flowering season.

A colour-coordinated early-summer planting of lime-tolerant lilac and *Deutzia* × *hybrida* 'Mont Rose'.

Potentillas are made for chalk, and have a very long flowering season. *Potentilla fruticosa* 'Abbotswood' has pure white flowers and grey-green foliage and 'Primrose Beauty' is an old favourite, with soft-yellow, buttercup-shaped flowers in summer and autumn. The colour is intensified in shade and tends to bleach in sun.

Planting on chalky soil

If the soil is shallow, it can be hard to establish large, deep-rooted flowering shrubs, so take extra care when planting. Dig out a deep planting hole into the chalk bedrock, so the roots can spread out. And improve the water-holding capacity of chalky soils by adding plenty of well-rotted organic matter.

More shrubs for chalky soil

Choisya ternata
Cistus × *pulverulentus* 'Sunset'
Cotoneaster franchetii
Deutzia × *elegantissima* 'Rosealind'
Hebe 'Mrs Winder'
Hibiscus syriacus 'Hamabo'
Hypericum 'Hidcote'
Mahonia japonica
Philadelphus 'Belle Etoile'
Spiraea 'Arguta'
Syringa vulgaris 'Charles Joly'
Tamarix ramosissima 'Pink Cascade'
Teucrium fruticans
Weigela 'Florida Variegata'

Season by season

Once flowering shrubs have become established, pruning is perhaps the most important task to carry out at the right time – get it wrong and you could spoil the display for the following year and you may even kill the plant that you're trying to improve. It's good to be reminded when is the best time to propagate flowering shrubs, and when to be on the look-out for signs of pests and diseases so that any necessary action can be taken promptly. It's also useful to have a memory jogger for when to do other routine but essential tasks, such as mulching and protecting vulnerable plants from frost.

Spring

The days are warming up, the garden is waking up, and suddenly there's lots to be done. Pruning is an important job in the spring, with some shrubs requiring cutting back before they break into growth and others benefiting from pruning as soon as they've finished flowering. It's also a busy time for planting new additions to your borders, including evergreens, as well as feeding established shrubs.

Protection

If a severe spell of frosty weather is forecast, protect the new growth of vulnerable shrubs, such as sun roses (*Cistus*), by covering them with a double layer of garden fleece.

Pruning and maintenance

Shrubs that flower in early spring, such as forsythia, can be pruned once they've finished flowering, so the shrub has as much time as possible to put on the growth that will flower the following year. Feed and water after pruning.

Shrubs that flower in late summer, such as *Buddleja davidii*, *Caryopteris*, *Hydrangea paniculata*, *Lavatera* and *Perovskia*, produce their main crop of flowers on new growth; if you have not already cut back last year's growth (*see* page 123), you should do so now, just before the new shoots start to break. You can now trim summer-flowering heathers to remove the old flowerheads that were left to provide protection for the plant over the winter months.

When the show is over: forsythias should be pruned once the flowers have died back, in late spring.

The displays of early-flowering shrubs can be improved by routine dead-heading. Take care with camellias, rhododendrons and magnolias, because they produce the next year's flowers just below this year's fading blooms – so make sure that you break off the heads carefully. By mid-spring, the flowers on winter-flowering heathers will have faded and can be trimmed.

If you want to reduce the overall size of an evergreen shrub, cut back all of the main stems to a suitable actively growing sideshoot lower down. However, do not cut back into bare wood, because many evergreens will not resprout. Any early-flowering evergreen shrubs, including rhododendrons and

Early spring is the time to cut back shrubs that will be flowering in late summer, including *Buddleja davidii*.

Improve the framework of mature shrubs that have grown out of shape, like this camellia, by pruning out branches once the flowers are over.

Feeding

If your soil is impoverished, apply a general, well-balanced fertilizer around established flowering shrubs and hedges. How much you apply will depend on your soil type and its condition, so check the instructions. Feed container plants too, by inserting a slow-release fertilizer tablet that will provide nutrients for the whole growing season.

Mulching

Whenever you get the chance, top up loose mulches, so that they are 5–8cm (2–3in) deep over the root area of all flowering shrubs. In the case of acid-loving plants, such as camellias and rhododendrons, use a lime-free organic mulch, such as well-rotted garden compost or farmyard manure. Heather beds can be mulched with composted bark chippings to show off the plants to best effect.

Acid-loving shrubs need only a light feed of ericaceous fertilizer, sprinkled on the soil surface.

Pest control

If the leaves of evergreen flowering shrubs, such as rhododendrons, camellias and skimmias, are being notched and nibbled, go out after dark with a torch to see if you can find any vine weevil adult beetles and destroy them. Try to encourage natural predators, or apply a biological control (*see* page 73).

Propagating

You can make new plants by layering suitably low, flexible stems of several flowering shrubs, including camellias, rhododendrons and azaleas, wintersweet (*Chimonanthus*), witch hazels (*Hamamelis*), magnolias and pieris (*see* page 70).

camellias, that have grown unevenly and are lopsided, as well as those that have outgrown their allotted space, can be pruned in late spring, once they have finished flowering.

Planting

Provided the soil is not overly wet or frozen solid after overnight frosts, early spring is an ideal time to plant hardy, container-grown deciduous shrubs, and the last chance to plant bare-root shrubs. Evergreens, such as rhododendrons, that have outgrown their allotted space can be transplanted now.

In late spring, once the soil has warmed up a bit and the danger of frost has passed, you can plant all types of new evergreen shrubs, both root-balled and container-grown, so that they have time to get well established before the winter.

Spring is a busy time for planting new additions to your borders: here, a young lilac is being watered in.

Summer

Summer is when you want to spend time just enjoying your garden. If it's a long, dry one, however, you're likely to have some watering to do, and this is not the season to relax on the pests and diseases front. Some shrubs will need a prune once they've finished flowering, and it's a good time to take cuttings if you want to grow more of your favourite shrubs.

Relax and enjoy: *Ceanothus × pallidus* 'Marie Simon' flowers in late summer and needn't be pruned till late winter.

Watering and feeding

You shouldn't need to use precious water on established shrubs, except in periods of severe drought, but newly planted or repositioned shrubs will have to be watered regularly unless there is plentiful rain. It's important that the root zone is thoroughly soaked – watering little and often encourages shallow rooting and makes the plant more susceptible to drought in the future. Routinely check shrubs planted in demanding sites, such as on dry banks, among trees and beside hedges, to see if they need watering.

Never allow any flowering shrubs in containers to go short of moisture. If a slow-release fertilizer was not added to the compost during the spring, use a liquid feed once a fortnight.

Propagating

Propagating from cuttings can be a cheap way of producing lots of plants of the same shrub, perhaps for a new hedge or for ground cover. You can also insure against winter losses by taking a few cuttings from not-so-hardy flowering shrubs. Semi-ripe cuttings can be taken from early summer onwards, once the new growth has begun to go woody. Take them at the 'heel', where the sideshoot meets the stem.

If you're raising flowering shrubs from seed or from rooted cuttings, check regularly to make sure they're not becoming overcrowded. Pot up the seedlings individually as soon as they're large enough to handle safely, and the cuttings once they're well rooted. (*See also* pages 67–71.)

Pest patrol

Many pests and diseases are at their most active during the summer months. Keep an eye out for any aphids in the growing-tips of vulnerable shrubs and scrutinize plants for signs of mildew and leaf spots. Take prompt remedial action (*see* pages 72–5).

Pruning

Prune late spring or early summer flowering shrubs, if required, once they have finished flowering. Cut one in three of the oldest stems back to a newer shoot lower down or to a plump outward-facing bud. Semi-informal hedges, such as berberis, escallonia and lavender, can also be trimmed once the flowers are over.

Many deciduous flowering shrubs, like philadelphus, should be cut back once flowering is over, so summer is a busy time in the pruning calendar.

Autumn

Protecting any vulnerable flowering shrubs before the onset of the coldest weather is a priority as soon as you sense that autumn chill in the air. It is also an ideal time to plant new shrubs, try your hand at growing new plants from seed and generally play at catch-up on other tasks – including sweeping up all those leaves.

Protecting your plants
Early frosts can take you by surprise. Move any borderline-hardy shrubs planted in containers to a sheltered spot, perhaps by the garage or at the base of a hedge. Alternatively, wrap them in bubble wrap and horticultural fleece (*see* page 59).

Protect individual not-so-hardy flowering shrubs, such as evergreen

Abelia x *grandiflora* matures into an attractive shrub with the bonus of pink and white flowers in autumn.

The leaves you gather now will by next year have become a useful soil improver and garden mulch.

ceanothus and phygelius, from the damaging effects of cold winter winds with a layer of windbreak netting fabric or horticultural fleece. Other vulnerable shrubs may need their tops and roots protected too.

Planting new shrubs
Provided the soil is moist, this is an ideal time to plant container-grown shrubs. The soil will still be warm, so the new plants will root and have a chance of getting properly established by spring.

Making new plants
Layered shoots from flowering shrubs prepared last year will have rooted and can be severed from their parent plants. Pot them in loam-based compost or move them to well-prepared soil elsewhere.

Some flowering shrubs, such as brooms (*Cytisus*) and bottlebrush (*Callistemon*), can be grown from

seed. Choose a dry day to pick the ripening seedpods and put them into labelled paper bags; the pods will split and release the seeds.

Thin, trim, sweep, mulch
If necessary, thin out and tidy up autumn-flowering shrubs after flowering by cutting out one stem in three, starting with the oldest. In mild areas, summer-flowering heathers can be trimmed. Elsewhere, however, they are best left until early spring, so the faded flower spikes can provide some protection over the winter months.

Collect up fallen leaves from lawns and other areas of the garden and turn them into leaf mould. You can either fill perforated black polythene bags and stash them out of sight behind the garden shed or, if you're going to have a large quantity of leaves, create a special enclosure.

If you didn't get around to it in the spring, top up loose mulches of well-rotted organic matter, so that they are 5–8cm (2–3in) deep over the root area of all flowering shrubs.

Winter

The garden is lying dormant, but there's plenty to keep you busy: planting bare-root shrubs, moving deciduous shrubs, preparing beds for spring planting, taking cuttings and maybe doing a spot of renovation pruning.

Planting and replanting

If, during the dormant season, you buy any deciduous flowering shrubs bare-root, plant them at once or, if the soil is too wet or frozen, 'heel' them into a shallow trench in a sheltered part of the garden until conditions improve.

A deciduous shrub that has outgrown its allotted space, or is simply in the wrong spot, can be moved while dormant. Prepare the new site, including the planting hole, beforehand, so it can be moved with minimum disturbance.

After frost or gales, check all your newly planted shrubs to make sure

Winter is the ideal time to prepare new beds. Dig over thoroughly and remove weeds and other debris.

A colourful late-winter scene: the ericas will need a light trim in spring, when they have finished flowering.

their rootballs haven't been lifted by wind rock or frost action. Re-firm the soil where necessary.

If you're planning any new beds, get a head start and prepare them now, for planting in spring. Dig them over thoroughly, incorporating plenty of well-rotted organic matter. On heavy clay soils, leave large clods of earth to be broken down by frost action over the winter.

Taking cuttings

Winter is also an ideal time to take hardwood cuttings from flowering shrubs such as *Buddleja*, *Ribes*, *Sambucus* and *Weigela* (*see* pages 67–8). For next to nothing, you could even create a new flowering hedge by inserting a line of hardwood cuttings into prepared ground. Suitable shrubs would be *Forsythia* or *Ribes*, both of which root easily. One snag: you have to be prepared for the plants to take a few years to reach hedge height!

Pruning and renovating

Renovate overgrown deciduous shrubs while dormant. Shrubs that respond well to hard pruning can be cut down to a knee-high stubby framework. Or, follow the four-step process described on page 65.

In late winter in mild areas, you can prune late summer flowering shrubs, such as *Buddleja davidii*, which produce their main crop of flowers on new growth. Elsewhere, wait until early spring. Remove any old, unproductive wood before reducing the main stems by about two thirds. (*See also* pages 62–3.)

If necessary, thin winter-flowering shrubs after flowering, cutting out one stem in three (the oldest first).

Help wildlife

Encourage birds to visit your garden during the winter months by hanging birdfeeders in tall shrubs. While the birds wait their turn to feed, they will search out and devour overwintering pests, thereby reducing potential problems for the following year. You can also encourage hedgehogs to overwinter in your garden by leaving piles of leaves at the base of hedges or in the border in which they can hibernate. In spring they will reward you by eating lots of slugs.

Index

Page numbers in *italics* refer to plants illustrated and/or described in the A–Z of recommended flowering shrubs.

A

Abelia 22, 71
  A. 'Edward Goucher' 44
  A. × *grandiflora* 44, 112, 122
    A. × *g.* 'Francis Mason' 34, 44, *77*
Abeliophyllum distichum 44, 71, *77*
Abutilon 65, 69, 71
  A. 'Kentish Belle' 34, *77*
  A. megapotamicum 34, *77*
  A. × *suntense* 'Jermyns' 111, 112
Acacia 61
  A. dealbata 26
acidic soil 29, 41, 49, 115, 116
alkaline soil 49, 117
alpine heath *see Erica carnea*
Amelanchier lamarckii 26, 43, 45, 74, 115
Andromeda polifolia 71, *78*, 115
aphids 72, 121
Aralia elata 26, 34
Arbutus 61
  A. unedo 26
arching shrubs 44
architectural shrubs 25
Arctostaphylos uva-ursi 44, 71, *78*
Aucuba japonica 109, 114
autumn colour 44
autumn tasks 122
Azalea 12, 19, 33, 35, 38, 53, 63, *100*, 120
Azara dentata 26

B

banks and slopes 15, 110
barberry *see Berberis*
beauty bush *see Kolkwitzia amabilis*
Berberis 16, 38, 61, 71, 75, 121
  B. darwinii 16, 33, 44, 45, 65, *78*, 111, 114
  B. julianae 43
  B. × *stenophylla* 25, 33, 44, 45, 114
  B. thunbergii 12–13, *78*
    B.t. 'Admiration' 43
    B.t. f. *atropurpurea* 'Nana' 14, 15, 110
    B.t. 'Bagatelle' 30
    B.t. 'Dart's Red Lady' 30
    B.t. 'Helmond Pillar' 30
  B. verruculosa *78*
bird and insect damage 75
blue flowering shrubs 29
bluebeard *see Caryopteris* × *clandonensis*
blueblossom *see Ceanothus thyrsiflorus*
bog rosemary *see Andromeda polifolia*
borders
  background shrubs 13, 21, 42
  border plans 40–2
  colours, working with 28–35
  depth 20
  designing 20–1
  mixed borders 10–11, 20–1
  narrow 43
botrytis 74
Brachyglottis 71
  B. Dunedin Group 'Sunshine' 45, *78*
Brazilian bellflower *see Abutilon megapotamicum*
bridal wreath *see Spiraea* 'Arguta'
broom *see Cytisus; Genista*
Buddleja 11, 14, 16, 17, 22, 30, 47, 62, 71, 73, 75, 123
  B. alternifolia 30, 44, 45, *79*
  B. davidii 63, 117, 119, 123
    B.d. 'Black Knight' 30, 31, 45, *79*
    B.d. 'Royal Red' 44
    B.d. 'White Profusion' 45
  B. globosa 34, *79*
  B. 'Lochinch' 30, *79*, 111
  B. 'Nanho Purple' 117
  B. × *weyeriana* 'Golden Glow' 23
buffalo currant *see Ribes odoratum*
bulbs, underplanting with 36–7, 41–2
Bupleurum fruticosum 71, *79*, 111
bush clover *see Lespedeza thunbergii*
bush honeysuckle *see Diervilla* × *splendens*
butterfly bush *see Buddleja*
butterfly lavender *see Lavandula pedunculata*
Buxus sempervirens 'Elegantissima' 42

C

calico bush *see Kalmia latifolia*
California lilac *see Ceanothus*
Callistemon 65, 71, 122
  C. citrinus 35
    C.c. 'Splendens' 43, *79*, 111, 112
Calluna vulgaris 70, 71, 75, *80*, 110, 116
  C.v. 'Dark Star' 15, *80*
  C.v. 'Golden Carpet' 44
  C.v. 'Robert Chapman' 43
Camellia 14, 18, 19, 33, 38, 40, 42, 48, 49, 53, 54, 56, 61, 64, 71, 72, 73, 74, 119, 120
  C. japonica 50, *81*, 116
    C.j. 'Adolphe Audusson' 43, *81*
    C.j. 'Alba Simplex' 109
    C.j. 'Elegans' 45, *81*
    C.j. 'Nuccio's Gem' 43
  C. 'Leonard Messel' 41, *81*
  C. sasanqua 'Narumigata' 23, *81*
  C. × *williamsii* *81*
    C. × *w.* 'Donation' *81*, 116
    C. × *w.* 'Jury's Yellow' 44
Cantabrian heath *see Daboecia cantabrica*
capsid bugs 72
Caragana arborescens 71, *81*
Carpenteria californica 71
  C.c. 'Ladham's Variety' *81*
Caryopteris 29, 62, 63, 71, 119
  C. × *clandonensis*
    C. × *c.* 'First Choice' 43
    C. × *c.* 'Heavenly Blue' *82*
caterpillars 72
Ceanothus 29, 54, 63, 64, 65, 71, 73, 75, 122
  C. arboreus 'Trewithen Blue' 29, *82*
  C. 'Autumnal Blue' 33, 45, *82*
  C. 'Blue Mound' 44, *82*
  C. 'Burkwoodii' 33, *82*
  C. 'Concha' 12, 43, *82*, 111
  C. × *delileanus* 'Gloire de Versailles' 23, 45, *82*
  C. griseus var. *horizontalis* 'Yankee Point' 15, 110
  C. × *pallidus* 'Marie Simon' 121
  C. 'Puget Blue' 44, *82*, 111, 112
  C. thyrsiflorus *82*
    C.t. 'Skylark' 38, 45, *82*
    C.t. var. *repens* 44, *82*, 110
Ceratostigma 29, 71
  C. griffithii *83*
  C. willmottianum 17, 44
    C. w. 'Forest Blue' 29, *83*
Cercis siliquastrum 26, 27
chalky soil 48, 117
Chimonanthus praecox 22, 44, 71, *83*, 120
Chinese lantern *see Abutilon*
Choisya 14, 16, 19, 22, 23, 33, 38, 61, 65, 71, 73, 75
  C. × *dewitteana* 'Aztec Pearl' 42, 44, *83*
  C. ternata 33, 34, 44, 45, 113, 117
    C.t. 'Sundance' 24, 44, *83*
choosing and buying shrubs 50–1
Christmas box *see Sarcococca*
cinquefoil *see Potentilla*
Cistus 16, 40, 50, 61, 64, 65, 71, 111, 119
  C. × *argenteus* 'Peggy Sammons' 84
  C. × *beanii* 44
  C. × *dansereaui* 'Decumbens' 45
  C. 'Elma' 111
  C. × *hybridus* 43, *84*
  C. × *lenis* 'Grayswood Pink' 31, 40, *84*
  C. obtusifolius 'Thrive' 44, 111
  C. × *pulverulentus* 'Sunset' *84*, 111, 117
  C. × *purpureus* 45
    C. × *p.* 'Alan Fradd' *84*
clay soil 48, 49, 113, 116, 123
Clerodendrum 71
  C. bungei *84*
  C. trichotomum var. *fargesii* 26
Clethra 61, 71
  C. alnifolia 43, 115
    C.a. 'Paniculata' 44, *85*
climbing plants, growing through shrubs 38–9
cold, sunless sites 43
colour 28–35
Colutea arborescens 26
common bearberry *see Arctostaphylos uva-ursi*
companion planting 36–9
compost 49
containers 18–19, 43, 52–3
  feeding 19, 53, 120, 121
  plant selector 43
  planting 19, 52–3
  pruning 64
  repotting 19, 53
  winter protection 59
Convolvulus cneorum 43, 44, 45, 71, *85*, 112
coral spot 74
Cornish heather *see Erica vagans*
Cornus 73, 75
  C. alba 43, 115
  C. canadensis 44
  C. 'Eddie's White Wonder' 26, 32
  C. florida
    C.f. 'Cherokee Chief' 43
    C.f. 'Sunset' 44
  C. kousa 61
    C.k. var. *chinensis* 26, 27, 38, 43, 116
    C.k. 'Miss Satomi' 44
  C. mas 26, 27, 34, 44
    C.m. 'Variegata' 44
  C. 'Porlock' 44
Corokia cotoneaster 71, *85*, 112
Coronilla 65, 71
  C. valentina subsp. *glauca* 43
    C.v. subsp. *g.* 'Citrina' 34, *85*, 111
Corylopsis 61, 71
  C. pauciflora 34, *85*, 116
Corylus
  C. avellana 'Contorta' 26

C. maxima 'Purpurea' 30
Cotinus 74
  C. coggygria 'Royal Purple' 26, 30, 35
Cotoneaster 14, 16, 71, 73, 74, 113
  C. dammeri 44, 110
  C. franchetii 85, 113, 117
  C. frigidus 'Cornubia' 44, 45
  C. horizontalis 43, 44, 45
  C. lacteus 43
  C. simonsii 12
  C. × watereri 'John Waterer' 26
cotton lavender *see Santolina*
Crataegus 16
crimson bottlebrush *see Callistemon citrinus*
cross-leafed heath *see Erica tetralix*
cucumber mosaic virus 75
cutting, shrubs for 44
cuttings 67–9, 121, 123
  hardwood 67, 68
  semi-ripe 68, 69, 121
  softwood 69
  stem-tip cuttings 69
Cytisus 14, 22, 34, 54, 64, 65, 71, 75, 122
  C. battandieri 14, 26, 44, 111
  C. 'Burkwoodii' 86
  C. × kewensis 15, 86
  C. 'Minstead' 112
  C. × praecox 112
    C. × p. 'Allgold' 34, 45, 86
    C. × p. 'Warminster' 34, 86
  C. scoparius 'Cornish Cream' 86

D

Daboecia 71, 116
  D. cantabrica subsp. *scotica* 'Silverwells' 43, 80, 86
daisy bush *see Olearia*
damp conditions 115
Daphne 14, 61, 71, 75
  D. bholua 42, 44, 86
    D.b. 'Darjeeling' 42, 86
    D.b. 'Jacqueline Postill' 22, 44, 86
  D. × burkwoodii 'Somerset' 40, 87
  D. mezereum 31, 43, 44, 87
  D. odora 34
    D.o. 'Aureomarginata' 87
  D. pontica 109
Darley dale heath *see Erica × darleyensis*
Desfontaina spinosa 71, 87, 116
Deutzia 62, 65, 69, 71, 117
  D. × elegantissima 'Rosealind' 31, 117
  D. × hybrida
    D. × h. 'Magicien' 45

D. × h. 'Mont Rose' 45, *87*, 117
D. × h. 'Strawberry Fields' 25, 44
D. × rosea 'Carminea' 44
D. scabra 'Plena' 44
Diervilla × splendens 23, 71, *87*
Dipelta floribunda 71, 88
dogwood *see Cornus*
dome- and mound-forming shrubs 25, 44
downy mildew 74
Drimys winteri 26
drought 75
drought-tolerant shrubs 45, 111

E

eelworms 72–3
elder *see Sambucus*
Embothrium coccineum 26, 116
Enkianthus campanulatus 26, 44, 116
Erica 71, *79*, 116
  E. arborea var. *alpina* 12, 112
    E.a. var. *a.* 'Albert's Gold' 88
  E. carnea 88, 110
    E.c. 'Challenger' 31, 88
    E.c. 'Myretoun Ruby' 15, 88
    E.c. 'Springwood White' 15, 41, 44, 80, 88, 110
    E.c. 'Vivelli' 43, 88
  E. × darleyensis 44
    E. × d. 'Ghost Hills' 30
    E. × d. 'J.W. Porter' 88
  E. tetralix 'Pink Star' 88
  E. vagans 'Lyonesse' 89
Escallonia 13, 16, 33, 42, 61, 65, 71, 73, 121
  E. 'Apple Blossom' 12, 89, 111
  E. bifida 24
  E. 'Iveyi' 45, 89
  E. 'Pride of Donard' 45
  E. 'Red Hedger' 43
  E. rubra
    E.r. 'Crimson Spire' 43
    E.r. var. *macrantha* 17
Eucryphia × nymansensis 'Nymansay' 26, 116
Euonymus fortunei 'Emerald 'n' Gold' 109
evergreen shrubs 24, 33, 36, 45, 59, 63–4
Exochorda × macrantha 'The Bride' 32, 41, 44, 71, 89

F

Fabiana imbricata 32, 71, 89
fast-growing shrubs 45
Fatsia japonica 24, 25, 38, 44, 71, 89, 109
feeding 56, 120, 121

fertilizers 56, 120
fireblight 74
flea beetles 72
flower shapes 23
flowering currant *see Ribes*
flowering shrubs
  characteristics 9
  choosing and buying 50
  colours 28–35
  companion planting 36–9
  in containers 18–19, 43, 52–3
  evergreen shrubs 24, 33, 36, 45, 59, 63–4
  feeding 56, 120, 121
  mixed borders 10–11, 20–1, 40–2
  moving 54, 123
  planting 51–3, 120, 122, 123
  scent 22, 44
  structure and form 9, 11, 23–5
  sub-shrubs 25
  tree-like shrubs 15, 26–7
  using 10–15
  watering 55, 121
  for wildlife 13, 16–17, 123
focal points 10, 43
foliage
  colourful 24, 30, 34, 44
  evergreen 45
  leaf shapes 23–4
  variegated 28, 44
Forsythia 11, 44, 61, 62, 68, 71, 72, 75, 113, 119, 123
  F. × intermedia
    F. × i. 'Lynwood Variety' 34, 43, 89
    F. × i. 'Spectabilis' 45
    F. × i. 'Week-End' 43, 113
Fothergilla major 44, 61, 71, 90
fountain-shaped shrubs 24–5
Fremontodendron 71, 111
  F. 'California Glory' 14, 34, 90
French lavender *see Lavandula pedunculata*
frost 9, 51, 59, 75, 119, 122
frost pockets 114
fruits and berries 13, 16, 33, 44
Fuchsia 9, 50, 63, 66, 69, 71, 73, 75
  F. 'Firecracker' 35
  F. 'Genii' 117
  F. magellanica 12, 13, 45
  F. 'Mrs Popple' 44, 90
  F. 'Riccartonii' 14, 41, 43, 45, 90, 117
  F. 'Tom Thumb' 43, *90*
fungal diseases 74, 75

G

galls 72
gap-fillers 14

Garrya 71
  G. elliptica 'James Roof' 14, 33, *90*
Gaultheria procumbens 15, 41, 44, 71, *90*, 110
Genista 71
  G. hispanica 90, 111
  G. lydia 15, 43, 44, *91*, 110, 112
  G. pilosa 'Vancouver Gold' 34
glory flower *see Clerodendrum*
gorse *see Ulex europaeus*
grafting 70
grey mould 74
ground cover
  annual plants 38
  perennial plants 37–8
  shrubs 14–15, 25, 44, 110
guelder rose *see Viburnum opulus*

H

Halesia carolina 12, 26, 27
× Halimiocistus 71
  × H. 'Ingwersenii' 43, 45, *91*, 112
  × H. sahucii 44
Hamamelis 22, 24, 34, 61, 62, 71, 120
  H. × intermedia 50, *91*
    H. × i. 'Arnold Promise' 43, *91*
    H. × i. 'Jelena' 44, *91*
    H. × i. 'Pallida' *91*, 116
heaths and heathers 14, 16, 40 *see also Calluna; Erica*
Hebe 19, 20, 25, 30, 33, 40, 59, 61, 65, 71, 74
  H. albicans 91
  H. 'Emerald Gem' 43
  H. 'Great Orme' 40, 45, *91*
  H. 'Midsummer Beauty' 45, *91*
  H. 'Mrs Winder' 42, 44, 117
  H. 'Pewter Dome' 43, *91*
  H. pinguifolia 'Pagei' 15, 38, 44, 45, *91*, 110
  H. rakaiensis 43, *92*
  H. 'Red Edge' 40, 44, *92*, 112
  H. 'Silver Queen' 43
  H. 'Watson's Pink' 17
hedges and dividers 12–13, 43
Helianthemum 16, 25, 63, 71, 110
  H. 'Amy Baring' 31, *92*
  H. 'Ben Fhada' 34, 35, *92*
  H. 'The Bride' 43
  H. nummularium 111
  H. 'Wisley Primrose' 44
herbaceous plants, treating shrubs as 9, 25
Hibiscus 29, 39, 61, 62, 71
  H. syriacus 50, 66
    H.s. 'Hamabo' 44, *92*, 117
    H.s. 'Oiseau Bleu' 45, *92*
Himalayan honeysuckle *see*

Leycesteria formosa
honey fungus 74
honeysuckle *see Lonicera*
horticultural fleece 59
hot, dry areas 111
humus 49
Hydrangea 10, 18, 20, 28, 29, 62, 69, 71, 73, 75, 115, 120
   H. arborescens 'Annabelle' 32, 43, *92*
   H. macrophylla 29, 43, 44, 50, *92*, 115
      H.m. 'Ami Pasquier' 43
      H.m. 'Ayesha' 31, *92*
      H.m. 'Mariesii Perfecta' 45
      H.m. 'Zorro' 43, 115
   H. paniculata 63, 66, 119
      H.p. 'Grandiflora' *93*
      H.p. 'Kyushu' 44
      H.p. 'Unique' 113
   H. 'Preziosa' 41, 44, *93*
   H. quercifolia 43
   H. serrata 'Bluebird' 45
Hypericum 71, 75
   H. androsaemum 43
   H. 'Hidcote' 23, 38, 45, *93*, 113, 117
   H. × inodorum 44
   H. olympicum f. *uniflorum* 'Citrinum' 43

I, J

indigo *see Indigofera heterantha*
Indigofera heterantha 44, 71, *93*
infill planting 51–2
iron and magnesium deficiency 75
Itea 71
   I. ilicifolia 21, *93*
   I. virginica 'Henry's Garnet' 44
Japanese angelica tree *see Aralia elata*
Japanese aralia *see Fatsia japonica*
Japanese barberry *see Mahonia japonica*
Japanese rose *see Kerria japonica*
Japanese skimmia *see Skimmia japonica*
Japanese snowball bush *see Viburnum plicatum*
Jasminum 73
   J. nudiflorum 14, 23, 34, 71, *93*
Jerusalem sage *see Phlomis fruticosa*
Judas tree *see Cercis siliquastrum*

K

Kalmia 71
   K. angustifolia f. *rubra 94*
   K. latifolia 94, 116
Kerria japonica 9, 14, 25, 71, *94*
   K.j. 'Golden Guinea' 45, *94*
   K.j. 'Pleniflora' 44, *94*, 113

Kolkwitzia amabilis 31, 44, 62, 65, 70
   K.a. 'Pink Cloud' 25, *94*
Korean lilac *see Syringa meyeri*
Korean spice viburnum *see Viburnum carlesii*

L

laurustinus *see Viburnum tinus*
Lavandula 13, 16, 22, 30, 40, 64, 65, 71, 112, 121
   L. angustifolia 66, 111
      L.a. 'Hidcote' 17, 43, *94*
      L.a. 'Imperial Gem' 44
      L.a. 'Loddon Blue' 43
      L.a. 'Munstead' 30, 45, *94*
      L.a. 'Royal Purple' 40, *94*
   L. × intermedia 44
      L. × i. 'Grosso' *94*
   L. pedunculata subsp. *pedunculata* 95
   L. stoechas 43
      L.s. 'Kew Red' 31
Lavatera 54, 63, 65, 71, 75, 119
   L. × clementii
      L. × c. 'Barnsley' 14, 31, 45, *95*
      L. × c. 'Rosea' 44
lavender *see Lavandula*
layering 70, 120, 122
leaf miners 73
leaf mould 58, 122
leaf shapes 23–4
leaf spots 74–5
Leptospermum scoparium 'Red Damask' 26, 31
Lespedeza thunbergii 25
Leucothoe fontanesiana 71, *95*
Leycesteria formosa 14, 44, 45, 69, 70, *95*, 115
lilac *see Syringa*
lily-of-the-valley shrub *see Pieris*
ling *see Calluna vulgaris*
Lithodora diffusa 'Heavenly Blue' 29
loam 48
long-flowering shrubs 23, 45
Lonicera 71
   L. fragrantissima 95
   L. × purpusii 16, 22, 44
      L. × p. 'Winter Beauty' 44, *95*
loppers 47
Lupinus arboreus 25

M

Magnolia 25, 30, 38, 39, 61, 62, 70, 71, 73, 74, 119
   M. grandiflora 'Exmouth' 45
   M. liliiflora 'Nigra' 41, *96*, 116
   M. × loebneri 'Leonard Messel' 26, 27
   M. × soulangeana 23, 26,

31, 116
      M. × s. 'Lennei' 21
   M. stellata 50, *96*
      M.s. 'Waterlily' 43, *96*
   M. 'Susan' 44, 116
Mahonia 11, 38, 42, 50, 61, 65, 71, 75, 109
   M. aquifolium 43
      M.a. 'Apollo' 36, 44, *96*, 110
      M.a. 'Smaragd' *96*, 109
   M. japonica 43, 44, 45, *96*, 117
   M. lomariifolia 45
   M. × media 25
      M. × m. 'Charity' 45, *96*, 109, 113
      M. × m. 'Winter Sun' 43, *96*
mallow *see Lavatera*
manure 49
marsh andromeda *see Andromeda polifolia*
Mexican orange blossom *see Choisya*
mixed borders 10–11, 20–1
mock orange *see Philadelphus*
moisture-loving shrubs 115
moving shrubs 54, 123
mulching 55, 58, 120, 122
multi-stemmed specimen shrubs 27
multi-tasking shrubs 40–1
myrtle *see Myrtus communis*
Myrtus communis 22, 44, 45, 71
   M.c. subsp. *tarentina 96*

N, O

New Zealand tea tree *see Leptospermum scoparium*
Olearia 65, 71
   O. × hastii 97, 111
   O. macrodonta 26, 43, 112
   O. × scillioniensis 'Dorrien-Smith' 43
orange ball tree *see Buddleja globosa*
Oregon grape *see Mahonia aquifolium*
Osmanthus 71
   O. × burkwoodii 97
   O. delavayi 38, 44, *97*, 113
      O.d. 'Pearly Gates' 22
   O. heterophyllus 33, 34, *97*
      O.h. 'Gulftide' 45, *97*
      O.h. 'Variegatus' 42

P

Paeonia 71
   P. ludlowii 42, *97*
   P. suffruticosa 23, *97*
pea tree *see Caragana arborescens*
pearl bush *see Exochorda × macrantha* 'The Bride'
peaty soil 48, 49

periwinkle *see Vinca*
Perovskia 16, 22, 62, 63, 119
   P. 'Blue Spire' 25, 112
Persian lilac *see Syringa × persica*
pests and diseases 72–5, 120, 121
pH 29, 49
Philadelphus 11, 38, 41, 62, 65, 69, 71, 117, 121
   P. 'Beauclerk' 45
   P. 'Belle Etoile' 13, 25, 32, 44, *98*, 117
   P. coronarius 'Aureus' 24, 30, 34, 40, 42, 44, *98*
   P. 'Manteau d'Hermine' 14, 38, 44, *98*
   P. 'Minnesota Snowflake' 45
   P. 'Virginal' 44, *98*, 113
Phlomis
   P. fruticosa 43, 45, 71, *98*
   P. italica 98, 111
Phygelius 71, 122
   P. aequalis 'Yellow Trumpet' 23, *98*
   P. × rectus 'African Queen' *98*
Physocarpus opulifolius 'Diabolo' 30
Pieris 18, 19, 24, 38, 48, 53, 61, 71, 120
   P. floribunda 'Forest Flame' 43, *99*, 116
   P. japonica 99
      P.j. 'Carnival' 44
      P.j. 'Debutante' 44
      P.j. 'Katsura' 45
      P.j. 'Little Heath' 41, 43, *99*
pink flowering shrubs 31
Pittosporum tobira 26, 45
planting 51–3
   bare-root shrubs 52, 120, 123
   container-grown shrubs 51, 120, 122
   in containers 19, 52–3
   in open ground 51, 52
plants for a purpose 43–5
plumbago *see Cerastostigma*
pollution-tolerant shrubs 45
Potentilla 16, 25, 71, 117
   P. 'Abbotswood' 117
   P. arbuscula 50
   P. fruticosa
      P.f. 'Elizabeth' 14, 23, 34, 44, *99*
      P.f. 'Primrose Beauty' 45, 117
      P.f. 'Red Ace' 9
      P.f. 'Tilford Cream' 42, *99*
      P.f. 'Vilmoriniana' 43
      P.f. 'Tangerine' 35, *99*
   P. 'Gibson's Scarlet' 35
   P. 'Goldfinger' 45
   P. 'Medicine Wheel Mountain' 44
powdery mildew 75
propagation 67–71, 120, 121, 122